MICHELLE LEFEVRE, NA
JENNY LLOYD, RACHAEI
JERI DAMMAN, GILLIAN F   ̣. . . ᴎᴅ
CARLENE FIRMIN

INNOVATION IN
SOCIAL CARE

New Approaches for Young People Affected
by Extra-Familial Risks and Harms

POLICY PRESS SHORTS POLICY & PRACTICE

First published in Great Britain in 2024 by

Policy Press, an imprint of
Bristol University Press
University of Bristol
1–9 Old Park Hill
Bristol
BS2 8BB
UK
t: +44 (0)117 374 6645
e: bup-info@bristol.ac.uk

Details of international sales and distribution partners are available at
policy.bristoluniversitypress.co.uk

British Library Cataloguing in Publication Data
A catalogue record for this book is available from the British Library

ISBN 978-1-4473-7123-6 paperback
ISBN 978-1-4473-7124-3 ePub
ISBN 978-1-4473-7125-0 OA PDF

Cover design: Bristol University Press
Front cover image: iStock

Contents

List of figures and boxes

Figures

Boxes

Glossary

(Child) Criminal exploitation In the UK, this is defined as where a child or young person under the age of 18 (or a vulnerable adult) is coerced, manipulated or deceived into criminal activity (1) in exchange for something the victim needs or wants, and/or (2) for the financial advantage or increased status of the perpetrator or facilitator. It can occur either through physical contact or the use of technology.

Child protection This refers to a legal set of duties carried out by systems and practitioners to protect individual children identified as suffering or likely to suffer significant (serious) harm. It is part of the wider safeguarding role.

(Child) Sexual exploitation In the UK, this is defined as where a child or young person under the age of 18 (or a vulnerable adult) is coerced, manipulated or deceived into sexual activity (1) in exchange for something the victim needs or wants, and/or (2) for the financial advantage or increased status of the perpetrator or facilitator. It can occur either through physical contact or the use of technology.

Extra-familial risks and harms This refers to dangerous or harmful contexts and situations involving peers and adults unconnected to young people's families or home, which may be associated with exploitation, abuse or criminality, and that raise safeguarding concerns. Examples include: sexual and criminal exploitation and trafficking; peer-to-peer sexual and relational abuse; and serious physical violence between young people.

Interagency/multi-agency The terms 'multi-agency', 'interagency' and 'interdisciplinary' are used interchangeably to refer to any collaboration between agencies or between professionals from different agencies.

Peer-to-peer abuse This includes physical and sexual abuse, harassment and violence, and bullying, emotional harm and teenage relationship abuse. It may take place online and offline, and may extend to involvement in grooming other children for exploitation.

Safeguarding This is defined broadly in the UK as a collective responsibility to protect people's health, well-being and human rights, and enable them to live free from harm, abuse and neglect. Within the Children Act 1989 (England and Wales) and subsequent statutory guidance, safeguarding encompasses actions taken to promote the welfare of children and protect them from harm. 'Child protection' is a subset of safeguarding, referring to systems and roles dedicated to assessing and addressing risks and harms for young people under the age of 18, largely through interventions focused on parenting. For adults, statutory guidance under the Care Act 2014 describes safeguarding as protecting an adult's right to live in safety, free from abuse and neglect, including risk prevention.

Safeguarding adults boards In England, safeguarding adults boards are interagency networks that oversee and coordinate adult safeguarding arrangements across a locality within the remit of the Care Act 2014.

Social care 'Social care' is an umbrella term used within the UK to encompass the provision or brokering of services related to the care, protection or social or emotional support of children or adults defined (within primary legislation) as being in need of those services and/or at risk of harm without them (SCIE, 2012). We have used this broad definition to cover services and interventions delivered by organisations and practitioners within statutory, voluntary (non-profit) and community sectors to respond to extra-familial risks and harms.

Young people The term 'young people' refers to the individuals who are subject to, or involved with, the services for extra-familial risks and harms that are discussed in this book. Our broad definition of adolescence means that this includes children and young adults from the ages of 12 to 25. Although, in UK legislation, the term 'child' encompasses young people up to the age of 18, we reserve the use of 'child' in this book to refer to those below the age of 12.

Acknowledgements

This book would not have happened without the support of the Economic and Social Research Council. Its four years of funding for the Innovate Project enabled us to conduct the research upon which this book is based, gave us the time to write it and funded the open-access publication of the digital edition. We also acknowledge the additional financial support from the University of Sussex Library towards that open-access publication. We hope that this means the text will be shared widely in the practice field to facilitate the further development of services. We are grateful for the ideas shared by, and the many discussions with, other members of the Innovate Project not involved as authors of this book (Kristi Hickle, Reima Ana Maglajlic, Roni Eyal-Lubling, Carlie Goldsmith, Julie Temperley, Susannah Bowyer, Dez Holmes, Lisa Holmes and Rebecca Godar). We thank Delphine Peace and the anonymous external reviewer for their exceptionally thorough reviews of the whole manuscript, which enabled us to substantially improve our text and clarify our key messages. We acknowledge the particular contribution to this book of our learning partners – the professionals who allowed us into their sites of innovation to observe their practice and system developments in action, shared a range of data, and contributed many important perspectives during interviews and focus groups. We have learned so much from you and are grateful for everything you did to facilitate the data collection and analysis without which this book would not have been written. Finally, we draw attention to all the young people and parents whose lives and concerns were most affected by these practice and system innovations. The constraints of the pandemic meant that we did not achieve the kind of in-depth longitudinal engagement with you and your lived experience that we had originally envisaged, but we have sought throughout to hold you, as well as the potential impacts upon you of extra-familial risks and harms and innovation developments, at the centre of our thinking.

ONE

Setting the scene

Introduction

Innovation could scarcely be more zeitgeist. It is the framework of recourse for government, business, science and industry, which expect it to stimulate economic growth, turbocharge enterprise, address social, health and economic challenges, and deal with emergent challenges, such as climate change and pandemics. In the UK, where the research discussed in this book was conducted, the language of innovation is threaded through policy strategies, including for boosting investment, inspiring technological and medical invention, addressing energy needs, and dealing with the impacts of the COVID-19 pandemic (Department for Business, Energy and Industrial Strategy, 2021). It is hardly surprising, then, that social care organisations are also turning towards innovation to address trenchant social problems and improve services and interventions within a context of constrained resources.

The pursuit of innovation has engaged substantial investment of time and money from local and central government, charities, think tanks, consultancies, research bodies, and the practice field. The children's social care sector in England has perhaps been most captured by the paradigm. Since 2014 alone, the UK government has spent £333 million in support of innovation pilots, their evaluations and linked programmes of diffusion for promising approaches (National Audit Office, 2022). Such a high level of public investment is deemed to be merited when those in need of services reliably receive 'meaningful and effective help' to support them in challenging situations and protect them from complex risks (Department for Education, 2023: 16). The piloting and evaluation of new approaches to this end, and their scaling and spreading, grow apace in pursuit of more evidence-informed practice. To date, the primary focus of the majority of this literature has been on the effectiveness of new approaches for achieving aspired outcomes in response to specific problems and on the efficacy and value for money they offer within a constrained public funding milieu. As a result, there is now: increasing evidence about the approaches and interventions that are effective in supporting children, young people and families; a good grasp of the local and national factors that can act as barriers to innovation; and an emergent awareness of factors noted to be present when innovation succeeds in its aims (Brown, 2015; FitzSimons and McCracken, 2020). A better understanding is still required of how to stimulate and mobilise innovation in social care contexts, facilitate design and implementation, address sector-specific challenges, and support the scaling and spreading of promising approaches to new problems and contexts (Sebba et al, 2017). Indeed, even a shared definition of what is meant by 'innovation' in the social care context remains a work in progress (Hampson et al, 2021).

Responding to some of these questions is the focus of this book. Through a four-year research project in the UK funded by the Economic and Social Research Council – the Innovate Project (see: www.theinnovateproject.co.uk) – we have inquired into what happens when local authorities and social care organisations in the voluntary or independent sector embark on the process of innovation, either as sole agencies or when leading multi-agency partnerships. By studying processes of innovation as they unfolded in real time in six case-study sites in England and Scotland, we have been able to identify and explore factors that helped or hindered the process, including what mattered at different stages along the innovation journey, how decisions were made and ways in which risks and challenges related to the specific conditions of innovating within this sector were overcome (or not). In this first chapter, we set out our definition of innovation, provide further details of our study and outline what will be covered by the remaining chapters of this book.

What do we mean by 'innovation'?

When reviewing the literature in the first year of the Innovate Project, it quickly became apparent that there was no shared definition of what constitutes innovation in the social care sector. For example, across the tranche of project reports and evaluations emanating from the government-funded Children's Social Care Innovation Programme in England (Department for Education, 2022) – which formed the largest body of 'grey literature' identified by our review – the term was used rather freely to denote a range of approaches; these included the trialling of new practice methods, the adoption of models successful elsewhere, incremental practice improvement measures and wholescale (sometimes quite radical) system change.

The initial working definition of innovation that we adopted for the project was integrated from perspectives offered by the social innovation literature – in particular Murray et al (2010), Young Foundation (2012), Nesta (2016) OECD and Eurostat (2018) and Mulgan (2019) – and had five core elements:

- It is a new framework or model that is novel in the UK social care system, though it might have been adapted from implementation in a different discipline or country.
- It requires a radically different way of thinking and acting than generally found within conventional service structures and paradigms.

- Its introduction should enhance the operational capabilities of public and charitable sector organisations, improve collaborative relationships across agencies and with stakeholders, and result in more efficient use of assets and resources.
- Its ethos is participatory, strengths based and welfare oriented, aiming to support and empower marginalised children, young people, adults and communities.
- It is intended to produce more effective ways of working with individuals, families and groups than existing solutions, and is hypothesised to result in better outcomes for those individuals and groups; in the field of extra-familial risks and harms, this particularly includes improving young people's safety and well-being.

This definition proved useful and workable in enabling us to distinguish whether a new social care method, service or system should be classified as an example of innovation. Our exploration of some of the ethical challenges inherent to introducing innovation in certain circumstances (see Chapter Two) led us to distinguish a further characteristic that would allow an innovation to be described as trustworthy: that it adheres 'in process and implementation' to the ethical standards and principles of social work (Hampson et al, 2021: 209).

The context for our study

Innovation is a situated activity and so needs to be studied in context and over time if behaviours, dynamics and processes (both deliberate and unintended) are to be properly understood with reference to their impacts (Young Foundation, 2012). This consideration led us towards a longitudinal, multi-method, multiple case-study design (Hunziker and Blankenagel, 2021), which would enable us to observe activities and interactions in real time within local authorities, social care organisations and interagency safeguarding networks, and consider what was similar and different between six different sites of innovation. The context for our study was the introduction of new systems and interventions that were designed to support young people in negotiating risky and potentially harmful relationships, situations and environments encountered beyond the family home, and to address the effects of harm. We have previously grouped these unsafe social activities and contexts together under the term 'extra-familial risks and harms'; the category includes sexual and criminal exploitation, serious youth violence, and peer-to-peer harassment and abuse (Firmin et al, 2022).

Such risks and harms might be characterised as 'wicked problems' (Coliandris, 2015), as they have been difficult to address through conventional safeguarding and welfare systems, and rapidly evolve over time and place, both in how they manifest and in what they are understood to constitute. In the UK, for example, the sexual exploitation of children under the age of 16 was only properly constituted as a child protection concern, rather than a form of 'child prostitution', towards the end of the first decade of the 21st century (Department for Children, Schools and Families, 2009). In countries beyond the UK, criminal exploitation remains less established as a safeguarding concern, and the relatively recent emergence of a form of organised drugs distribution from urban to rural counties known as 'County Lines' appears quite specific to the UK (Coomer and Moyle, 2017). Professional systems across a range of countries also continue to struggle to balance young people's rights to voice, privacy and agency with concerns about their safety (Sapiro et al, 2016). Societies remain conflicted about the extent to which young people should be held responsible for their actions when exploitation is an issue; young people who have engaged in criminal behaviours simultaneous to their own victim experiences may receive only, or predominantly, a law-enforcement response in countries like England that silo child welfare and criminal justice at national policy and local practice levels (Radford et al, 2017).

Such complexities encourage statutory and voluntary sector organisations to turn to innovation to support them in experimenting with new approaches that can: better adapt to emergent social conditions; balance young people's needs, rights and preferences; work in collaboration with young people and families; and support practitioners in creative, but disciplined, risk taking. As we began the Innovate Project in 2019, three new frameworks for practice and system innovation committed to these principles were gaining increasing attention and traction in the social care sector: Trauma-informed Practice, Contextual Safeguarding and Transitional Safeguarding.

Not only were these three frameworks novel in their application within the social care field for addressing risks and harms beyond family contexts, but they also required a way of thinking and acting that was radically different to existing approaches, both towards young people and within/across organisational systems. Each offered a well-theorised premise for producing more effective ways of working with young people affected by extra-familial risks and harms, but little was known about how each framework might be implemented to best effect within the prevailing sector conditions. None of the three yet offered a manualised system or practice template to be operationalised with fidelity in new sites (as might be more in line with a standard 'diffusion' model for rolling out promising new approaches [see Rogers, 2003]). This was not only because the frameworks were still at the stage of early development or trialling but also because each was based on a set of principles that needed to be interpreted and tailored for each specific context. This fluidity and their emergent nature offered the potential for longitudinal learning about the processes of innovation as new systems and practice approaches unfolded within local authorities, interagency safeguarding networks and organisations in the voluntary or charitable sector. It was anticipated that the particularities of what each framework might demand in the way of local system capabilities and resources should also become apparent.

The three frameworks for practice and system innovation

We go on now to provide a short summary of each of the frameworks for practice and system innovation, signposting readers to other resources should they wish to investigate them further.

Trauma-informed Practice

Rooted in a fundamental understanding of the manifold ways in which the experience of trauma can affect individuals both immediately and more chronically through the lifespan, Trauma-informed Practice offers a framework for promoting a strengths-based way of working that builds trust, prioritises physical, emotional and relational safety, offers choice, avoids re-traumatising service users, and works collaboratively with service users to enable them to regain control and autonomy (Harris and Fallot, 2001; Sweeney et al, 2016; for a summary of Trauma-informed Practice, see also Box 1.1). The framework does not provide a template to be replicated by other services or any form of detailed information for implementation; rather, it offers points for consideration in service (re)design, so that its principles are tailored to specific contexts, service aims and system capabilities, and embedded within practice methods and systems.

Trauma-informed Practice was originally developed within the fields of psychology and mental health in the US and has more recently been considered relevant and useful for working with young people experiencing harms beyond the family home because it: recognises their needs for physical, emotional and relational safety (Shuker, 2013); respects their agency and rights (Lefevre et al, 2019); increases understanding of how they may be re-traumatised by systems meant to protect them (Beckett and Warrington, 2015); and seeks to ameliorate developmental trauma (Hickle and Lefevre, 2022). Originally conceived of as an approach to direct practice that would benefit traumatised service users, the application of Trauma-informed Practice has subsequently been extended to encompass the design of organisational systems and clinical supervision in ways that enable staff to remain emotionally engaged, develop resilience and avoid burnout (Bloom, 2005).

We selected two case-study sites in different areas of the UK that were just beginning to introduce Trauma-informed Practice into their safeguarding work with young people – a local authority and a children's trust – with each being responsible for the local delivery of statutory children's social care services. Our research in these two sites sought to address critical knowledge gaps identified by Hanson and Lang (2016) in relation to the following: (1) how change within a system is conceptualised, promoted and enacted through supervisory support for workers and through direct practice with children and young people; (2) how practice systems understand and interpret what a 'trauma-informed approach' means; (3) the resources required for effective implementation; and (4) the extent to which innovation on the basis of Trauma-informed Practice might result in practices better attuned to the needs of young people. As we began fieldwork, each site was in the early stages of applying the principles of Trauma-informed Practice in quite a modest way. Chapter Four details the divergent journeys taken by each site and what system components were needed to fully implement and embed the framework. An overview of Trauma-informed Practice is provided in Box 1.1.

BOX 1.1: AN OVERVIEW OF TRAUMA-INFORMED PRACTICE

What is it?

Trauma-informed Practice offers a set of principles that, when considered in the (re)design of interventions and systems, should both: (1) improve professional responses to people who have experienced trauma; and (2) support staff who are working with those individuals.

Why was it developed?

Trauma theory and the concept of post-traumatic stress had originally been applied to acute situations like natural disasters, accidents or wartime experiences. Harris and Fallot (2001) proposed a broader 'Trauma-informed Practice' following new insights into the traumatic impact on people who had experienced traumatic abuse and neglect in childhood ('developmental trauma') and/or repeated/multiple traumatic stressors over time ('complex trauma').

What are its principles?

The application of a trauma-informed framework in the field of extra-familial risks and harms (Hickle, 2019) proposes that practice methods and systems are designed around the following principles:

- recognising how developmental trauma impacts young people's capacity to manage impulses, regulate emotions, identify danger and assess for safe and healthy relationships;
- fostering trust through building relationships with young people that are reciprocal and interdependent;
- creating relational, physical and psychological safety for young people, intentionally seeking to avoid re-traumatising them during assessment and intervention;
- supporting young people to exercise choices that facilitate their safety, identify opportunities beyond risk and empower them towards a hopeful future; and
- understanding the wider contextual and political environments that contribute to young people's sense of unsafety in their worlds.

Applying the following additional principles in system design is necessary to supporting practitioners:

- understanding that working with traumatised people can lead to vicarious trauma for practitioners, and recognising signs and symptoms of trauma in workers;
- seeking to avoid (re-)traumatising staff in the course of their work;
- attending to relational practices throughout the service, particularly in the context of supervision, to build trust and create relational, physical and psychological safety for workers;
- ensuring workers have opportunities to exercise choice and control over working environments and work–life balance; and
- understanding the wider contextual and political environments that create emotional defences in staff and reduce their capacity to work in relational, trauma-informed and anti-oppressive ways (Bloom, 2005).

How has it been used?

Services based on Trauma-informed Practice have been emerging throughout the last 20 years across Global North countries (for example, the US, Canada, New Zealand, Australia, Norway, Sweden and the UK) and in numerous disciplines (Sweeney et al, 2016). The framework has been gaining increasing traction more recently in children's services in Scotland, with a policy 'Promise' to provide trauma-informed services, systems and workforces (The Promise, Scotland, 2020), and the issuing of a practice toolkit to implement this (Scottish Government, 2021). However, it remains a relatively new concept in the field of extra-familial risks and harms in the UK (Hickle, 2019).

Contextual Safeguarding

Developed by one of the authors of this book (Firmin et al, 2016; Firmin, 2017), Contextual Safeguarding began as a theoretical proposition that child protection systems needed to move beyond the traditional assumptions that risk of harm to a young person was necessarily attributable to action or inaction by their parents or carers, and that assessment and intervention should necessarily be family focused. Since the first pilot of a Contextual Safeguarding system in the London Borough of Hackney, funded by the Children's Social Care Innovation Programme in England, the diffusion of Contextual Safeguarding has moved apace. This has included formal trialling in nine local authority sites between 2019 and 2022 (Firmin and Lloyd, 2022), and a brief reference to the framework in the 2018 version of statutory guidance (Her Majesty's Government, 2018). This rapid progression along the innovation trajectory has occurred without any evidence yet having emerged of the effectiveness of this new framework for young people's safety and welfare outcomes, or for addressing risky contexts (Lefevre et al, 2020, 2023).

The framework of Contextual Safeguarding is innovative itself, in that it offers a new paradigm that unsettles the structure and family–oriented focus of child protection responses standard to the UK and other Global North countries. However, Contextual Safeguarding also requires innovation in its implementation, as interpreting and tailoring its principles and framework to a local context necessitates significant cultural, structural, procedural and practical changes within and across social care, wider interagency partnerships and local communities (Lefevre, 2023). One of the Innovate Project sites (a local authority children's social care department in England) drew on the framework to inform the development of a wider 'adolescent safety framework' across its region. The other – a pan-London charity supporting young people and their families, peers and communities affected by violence and exploitation – has been exploring the potential contributions of Contextual Safeguarding for organisations that do not hold statutory safeguarding responsibilities (see Peace, forthcoming).

Many of the authors of this book have been involved with the design (Firmin), delivery (Lloyd and Owens) or evaluation (Lefevre and Huegler) of the Hackney pilot of Contextual Safeguarding. As the second phase of evaluation in Hackney (Lefevre et al, 2023) overlapped with the timeline of the Innovate Project case studies, there has been a learning dialogue between the two. As a result, we have drawn additionally on innovation insights from the Hackney pilot at several points in this book, most notably, in Chapter Two, and have been explicit about this on each occasion. An overview of Contextual Safeguarding is provided in Box 1.2.

BOX 1.2: AN OVERVIEW OF CONTEXTUAL SAFEGUARDING

What is it?

Contextual Safeguarding offers a radical new way of structuring safeguarding systems so that they can assess and address the contexts beyond the home and family within which extra-familial risks and harms occur rather than solely seeking to change the behaviour of, or address risks with, individual young people (Firmin, 2020). Contextual Safeguarding is not a template model; instead, it offers a framework of principles and practice tools that need to be interpreted so that a new system design meets the particular needs of a local context.

Why was it developed?

This new perspective emerged from Firmin's review of cases of peer-to-peer abuse and violence which revealed that although young people involved in peer abuse often experienced significant harm, they did not generally receive a safeguarding response. This was because the conventional threshold for social care intervention had not been reached. Instead, parents were mostly tasked with keeping their children safe from future harm, and young people in conflict with the law tended to be dealt with by the youth justice system. The Contextual Safeguarding framework was elaborated to address these shortcomings (Firmin, 2017, 2018, 2020; Firmin et al, 2016; Firmin and Lloyd, 2020).

What are its principles?

Contextual Safeguarding systems should be designed around four innovative features that radically depart from conventional safeguarding approaches:

- systems and methods need to prevent, identify, assess and intervene with the social conditions that promote risk and perpetuate harm;
- extra-familial contexts should be incorporated into child protection frameworks;
- partnerships must be developed between all sectors and individuals responsible for the nature of extra-familial contexts; and
- outcomes of success should be measured in relation to contextual, as well as individual, change.

Full Contextual Safeguarding systems must operate at two levels: (1) 'contextual thinking' about extra-familial relationships, networks and locations should be incorporated into individual work with young people and families; (2) practices, systems and structures should enable identification, assessment and intervention with the contexts themselves in which young people are at risk of significant harm.

How has it been used?

The Hackney pilot sought to operationalise the theoretical framework into a new system that would revolutionise responses to extra-familial risks and harms. In 2019, emergent learning from the pilot led to the launch of a 'practice toolkit' to support other local authority areas in creating their own Contextual Safeguarding systems. This toolkit (see: www.contextualsafeg uarding.org.uk/toolkits/) has been further developed through subsequent projects, including formal trialling in nine local authority sites between 2019 and 2022 (Firmin and Lloyd, 2022). Over 80 local authorities and organisations in the UK and beyond are engaged in the development of their own Contextual Safeguarding systems.

Transitional safeguarding

Extra-familial risks and harms, as well as their effects and consequences, do not stop just because a young person reaches legal adulthood at age 18. Yet, social care and safeguarding systems for children and adults in the UK are based on very different legislative, policy and conceptual frameworks, themselves rooted in binarised conceptualisations of childhood and adulthood. Children are often deemed to have limited capacity to make decisions for themselves in the context of significant harm (Her Majesty's Government, 2018), while the framework for adult safeguarding in the Care Act 2014 prioritises an individual's rights, freedom, choice and control. This divergence between children's and adults' safeguarding systems insufficiently reflects the evidence that transitioning into adulthood is a process that extends well beyond the teenage years (Sawyer et al, 2018).

The concept of Transitional Safeguarding was coined by Holmes and Smale (2018) and elaborated on by Holmes (2022) as a way of inviting re-theorisation and innovation across children's and adults' safeguarding systems to enable them to respond in more developmentally attuned ways to young people's changing needs and avoid system 'gaps' around the age of 18. Again, Transitional Safeguarding does not offer a prescribed model; rather, it offers a 'joined-up approach to policy and practice', rooted in a framework of principles that requires conceptual, cultural and structural innovation at a local level (Office of the Chief Social Worker for Adults et al, 2021: 10).

As the Innovate Project began, the theorisation and operationalisation of the Transitional Safeguarding framework was still emergent, but the interest of a number of local authorities and interagency networks had been captured by the fresh perspective it offered. Including Transitional Safeguarding as one of our three innovation frameworks for study enabled us to learn more, in particular, about the early stages of innovation mobilisation and design. The nature of the two interagency sites in England we selected additionally offered insight into what might be facilitated or impeded by different forms of governances: one was led by the children's social care department in an urban unitary authority; the other was led by the safeguarding adults board in a metropolitan borough, working in collaboration with the local partnerships for children's safeguarding and community safety for that area. Neither site had ringfenced funding for their innovation.

By the end of our research involvement, developments in these two sites continued to remain at an early design phase. Both in these sites and in others within our wider Innovate Project Learning and Development Network of interested organisations and local authorities, the complexity of multidimensional and multi-agency whole-systems change was strongly apparent, with respect to both uncertainties (for example, about progress, pace, resourcing or governance) and the process of generative co-productive work. We discuss some of these complexities in Chapter Three. An overview of Transitional Safeguarding is provided in Box 1.3.

BOX 1.3: AN OVERVIEW OF TRANSITIONAL SAFEGUARDING

What is it?

Transitional Safeguarding is an emergent framework that aims to stimulate evidence-informed systemic change in local areas in order to improve safeguarding and support that better meets the needs of young people in transition to adulthood (Holmes and Smale, 2018; Holmes, 2022). Rather than offering a prescribed model, Transitional Safeguarding comprises a set of principles that need to be applied in different ways according to local circumstances with the aim of life-course-based 'whole-systems' change.

Why was it developed?

Currently, neither adult- nor child-oriented safeguarding systems focus sufficiently on the specific developmental and transitional needs of adolescents and young adults. This leads to differences and gaps between safeguarding services, policies and practice systems, which are designed with either children or adults in mind. An emergent formulation of Transitional Safeguarding was proposed to stimulate responses to the problems created by seeing childhood and adulthood as divergent ends of a spectrum. Transitional Safeguarding is concerned not only with extending protective services for children into early adulthood but also with incorporating principles that underpin the design of adult social care frameworks (for example, empowerment, choice and collaboration) into work with young people. 'Transitional' refers not only to human life stages but also to the boundary-spanning connections that are needed between local agencies, including social care, health, education and housing, their interface with youth and criminal justice agencies, and the services offered by the voluntary sector.

What are its principles?

Transitional Safeguarding proposes that new systems are designed around three intersecting core principles:

- they are ecological and contextual, using place-based perspectives;
- they are designed with developmental and transitional needs and strengths in mind, allowing for a more fluid alignment of systems and services across the life course; and
- they foreground relational perspectives, prioritising capacity-building and trauma-attuned approaches.

They are also designed around three cross-cutting themes:

- they are informed by a variety of evidence relevant to local issues and priorities – from data and research to practice wisdom and lived experience;
- they actively attend to equality, diversity and inclusion; and
- they are developed through co-production and other participative approaches that directly involve young people and their communities (Holmes, 2022; Office of the Chief Social Worker for Adults et al, 2021).

How has it been used?

Transitional Safeguarding principles are gaining traction and beginning to inform policy, systems and practice development across different areas and sectors in the UK, but its emergent character means that Transitional Safeguarding developments are ongoing.

Our research approach

It is notable that while the design and technological fields are open about innovations that do not 'take' (Mulgan, 2019), this does not seem to hold true in the social care sector. Our reviews of the innovation literature (Hampson et al, 2021; Lefevre et al, 2022) could find little detail of innovation projects that had struggled or foundered completely. This lack of openness is likely to relate to a pervasive blame culture in the public sector: services are worried not only about placing vulnerable families at risk if a new service 'does not work' but of being seen as having made errors or 'wasting' public money (Bason, 2018). As a result, the existing literature is not as useful as it could be in helping those leading and implementing innovation to recognise problems at the earliest stage and learn from what has not worked well elsewhere. Therefore, rather than considering what should be done in a given situation to achieve particular aims, our starting point in the Innovate Project was to look instead at what actually happened in real time and on the ground in the everyday contexts of six sites of innovation: local authorities, interagency safeguarding networks and organisations in the independent or charitable sector.

Data collection

Each of the frameworks for practice and service innovation (Trauma-informed Practice, Contextual Safeguarding or Transitional Safeguarding) was the focus of one of three separate research strands. Researchers worked across small teams in their strand to build relationships with key players in each site. A summary of the methods at the core of our ethnographic approach is set out in Box 1.4 (for a fuller account, see: www. theinnovateproject.co.uk/about-the-project/the-research-approach/). Our original intention had been for a form of 'embedded ethnography', where researchers would have been co-located with teams for several days at a time. However, the data-collection period spanned 2021–22 – in the midst of the COVID-19 pandemic and its attendant public health restrictions. As a result, the majority of data collection comprised interviews and observations of meetings conducted via video-calling software. Relatedly, we had also expected to observe and interview young people and parents involved with the designing and trialling of the innovations, but again, due to the impact of the pandemic, the sites were unable to involve and collaborate with service users in the ways that had been anticipated at the outset; as a result, we did not engage with young people and parents until the latter stages of the project.

BOX 1.4: THE DATA-COLLECTION METHODS AT THE CORE OF THE ETHNOGRAPHIC APPROACH

- Observations of strategic meetings in each of the six case-study sites to plan and review the design and implementation of the new intervention or system.
- Observations of multi-agency meetings held in each site to assess risk and plan safety for young people.
- 'Clarification discussions' with some of the individuals involved in those meetings to explore proceedings from their viewpoints.
- Interviews with leaders, managers and practitioners about their role, intentions and experiences during the innovation journey.
- Analysis of case-file documentation that revealed how professionals were thinking about young people and their approach to practice.
- Exploration of policy and practice guidance and performance indicators at a local and national level that were governing activities within the sites.

Our two-year ethnography was supplemented by knowledge-exchange activities conducted with our Innovate Project Learning and Development Network – senior professionals from other local authorities and organisations interested in innovation and/or the adoption of Transitional Safeguarding, Trauma-informed Practice or Contextual Safeguarding. As the theorisation of Transitional Safeguarding was still at an early stage, we undertook supplementary data collection to understand the wider national debates and policy developments that were emerging. This included: (1) interviews with expert informants, such as policy makers and sector leaders, who were contributing to the ongoing refinement of the framework (for example, Office of the Chief Social Worker for Adults et al, 2021); (2) national reflective group discussions for researchers and professionals involved in Transitional Safeguarding work; and (3) 'journey-mapping' interviews with professionals from our Learning and Development Network who were embarking on modest forms of system or practice change (see Chapters Three and Seven).

Data analysis

First and foremost, we constructed our research as case studies of innovation. These differed as to geographical context, type of governance (statutory or third sector), whether single- or multi-agency, and which of the three frameworks was providing a basis for innovation. Our method of analysis was informed principally by Institutional ethnography (Smith, 2005; Smith and Griffith, 2022); this approach looks closely at who is doing what, when, how and why. The aim is to surface what factors are at play when individuals and groups engage in particular activities under specific material conditions in the pursuit of particular goals, and the (intended and unintended) impacts of these. In this sense, the term 'institutional' refers not to the organisations and systems within which practitioners and managers do their everyday work but, rather, to the implicit and explicit forms of discourse, management, power and control that govern and organise their everyday work lives and practices (DeVault, 2006). These 'ruling relations' can only be discovered 'in motion', as they are brought into being in 'people's local doings, in particular sites and at particular times' (Smith, 2005: 68).

The researchers produced 'rich, thick empirical descriptions' of each piece of data as soon as possible after each event (Rankin, 2017: 5), indexing and mapping each item against others. This process illuminated connections and flows between organisational aspirations, social practices, policies, systemic constraints, institutional processes, power structures and discourses. Insights were produced at the micro-level (where power lay in individual sites), the meso-level (about ruling relations common to social care organisations) and the macro-level (discourses and expectations governing how young people are seen and responded to at a social and policy level with respect to vulnerability, risk, agency and value).

Ethical considerations

Ethical approval for the study was provided both by the University of Sussex and through local governance processes in the individual sites. While we could be confident that we were complying with standard ethical principles for research conduct (UK Research Integrity Office, 2023), we were troubled throughout by the extent to which we, as academic outsiders, might be making judgements and drawing inferences about the activities, motivations and subjectivities of hard-working and well-intentioned professionals. We did not consider ourselves to be standing above those whom we observed; indeed, many of us had grappled formerly with similar challenges as practitioners and social work managers ourselves. Our starting point was one of understanding and solidarity, recognising that we were just as influenced by the ruling relations of our society. Nonetheless, we were aware of the potential for judgementalism and sought from the start to incorporate our own project systems that would provoke our reflexivity about power and subjectivities as a matter of course.

To this end, we layered in psychosocial theories and group reflective methods to deepen our understanding of some of the complex human emotions, interactions and power dynamics not only that we witnessed but also that governed our own behaviours and analytic thinking (Salzberger-Wittenberg, 1983; Menzies-Lyth, 1988 [1959]; Ruch, 2007; Cooper and Lees, 2015). Over time, we came to see ourselves far less as researching outsiders than – using the lens of para-ethnography (Holmes and Marcus, 2008; Islam, 2015) – as journeying alongside our sites, which brought their own expertise to the analytic endeavour. We also grappled intensely with the ethical complexities of when and how to offer information, even advice, about innovation theory, extra-familial harm and the three frameworks. The complementary insights generated by these perspectives are discussed in Chapters Five and Seven.

About this book

Following on from this introduction, Chapter Two provides some overarching frameworks for understanding the processes of innovation in social care that have been developed through the Innovate Project's learning. In particular, it sets out what factors and processes can help facilitate innovation at different stages of the innovation journey. Chapters Three to Seven each discuss a key theme that emerged from data analysis. Chapter Three considers how revisiting earlier stages of design in recursive learning loops may be a normative characteristic of complex systems innovation rather than a mark of failure. Chapter Four explores the overlaps and contingencies between 'innovation' and practice improvement measures rather than the more common positioning of them as distinctive, even oppositional, entities. Chapter Five is about what 'works' in innovation but critiques standard quantitative or outcomes-focused notions of innovation 'success'. Chapter Six discusses the uncertainty and anxieties stirred up by innovation processes, and considers how these might be managed by system and project leaders. Chapter Seven focuses on the building of learning partnerships between researchers and innovators to facilitate contextually aligned and affectively attuned innovation. Finally, Chapter Eight considers the implications for policy and practice of the insights and frameworks presented in this book.

Conclusion

This chapter has set out in brief terms why this book is so necessary at the present time, that is, to respond to the gaps in current knowledge about the processes of innovation in social care through the description and analysis of situated innovation practice. The book will provide insights into how innovation might be facilitated and challenges overcome, drawn primarily from the Innovate Project's two years of ethnographic fieldwork in six case-study sites in the UK, which were developing new practice methods and systems to address extra-familial risks and harms using the frameworks of Trauma-informed Practice, Contextual Safeguarding or Transitional Safeguarding. However, the focus of this book is not the effectiveness of these three frameworks in addressing extra-familial risks and harms but, rather, the particularities of what each framework demands in the way of system capabilities, resources, relationships, ethics and policies in order to flourish and be sustained in a local context. Before we move to the five chapters that will each expand upon specific findings, we turn next in Chapter Two to outlining some conceptual frameworks about innovation practice that were developed through literature review and expert informant interviews in the early stages of the Innovate Project, and that have been tested for their salience through our fieldwork.

Key chapter insights for policy and practice

- Innovation can provoke the re-envisioning of existing paradigms and enable transformation of interventions and systems so that they address trenchant social problems and improve service experiences and outcomes within a context of constrained resources.
- More needs to be understood about the factors and processes that can stimulate innovation and enable it to flourish. Best use can then be made of public investment so that services offer value for money and their outcomes correspond with what young people and their families want.
- Contextual Safeguarding, Trauma-informed Practice and Transitional Safeguarding offer promising frameworks upon which practice and system innovation to address extra-familial risks and harms may be designed and delivered, but more needs to be learned about how they can be operationalised effectively in local contexts.

TWO

Creating the conditions for innovation to flourish

Introduction

In essence, innovation refers to new approaches that transform existing systems, interventions or paradigms in pursuit of new ways of thinking and acting that are better in some way than what went before. Within this simple definition are embedded a number of ethical and practical considerations that need to be addressed if the right system conditions are to be created that will enable innovation to flourish in a particular context. In this chapter, we discuss some of the features, dynamics and constraints that characterise the social work and social care context in the UK, particularly within the field of adolescent safeguarding. This discussion draws on a categorisation of 'foundational contextual domains' of innovation within which individual components may operate as barriers or enablers (see Figure 2.1). This categorisation was constructed through a framework analysis (Goldsmith, 2021) conducted in the first year of the Innovate Project, which integrated findings from a critical synthesis review of the literature with a thematic analysis of interviews with 20 expert informants – policy makers, academics, strategic leaders

Figure 2.1: Components of the foundational contextual domains that may facilitate or impede innovation

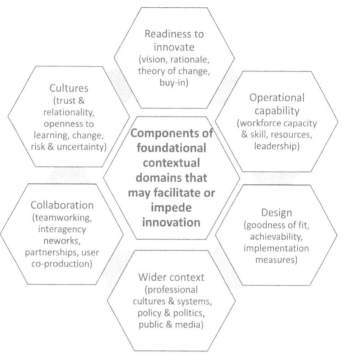

or practice leads in the social care field in the UK (see Lefevre et al, forthcoming). Each component might impede or facilitate the process of innovation, depending on the degree to which it has been taken into account in planning and operationalisation. Individual innovation journeys may be particularly affected by one, several or all components within these foundational contextual domains.

The following discussion of how these domains and their individual components influence the innovation process is structured with reference to our six-stage modelling of the innovation journey, which elaborates phases of: (1) mobilising; (2) designing; (3) developing; (4) integrating; (5) growing; and

(6) wider system change. This trajectory model was developed through the Innovate Project's knowledge synthesis of ten frameworks from the social innovation canon that have been drawn upon with some frequency within social care innovation projects and their evaluations (see Lefevre et al, 2022). Within each stage, we consider the ethical principles for planning and implementing social care innovation that we have previously outlined (Hampson et al, 2021), and raise questions for those funding and leading innovation initiatives to consider as part of project planning and review.

Considerations at different stages of the innovation journey

Getting ready to innovate

In the first stage of innovation – 'mobilisation' – organisations and networks begin to consider together the possibilities that a different way of operating might offer them. If innovation represents striving for something that works better than what went before, key questions are 'Better for whom?' and 'How?'. Answers to these questions will differ based on the views, status and lived experiences of those involved in system or service design, delivery or receipt. These individual positions and perspectives will shape why people might think a new approach is needed, what they hope an innovation might achieve and the parameters by which they judge its success. Young people and families, for example, commonly want interventions and systems that centre their concerns, are easy to access and treat them with care and respect. Practitioners are likely to be drawn towards new ideas or practice models that deepen understandings of specific dynamics of risks and harms, help them engage with families more productively, and offer the possibility of enhancing a young person's safety and well-being. While some service and system leaders may similarly be captured by a promising new design, others might be driven to innovate because a critical regulatory inspection means that 'staying still' is not an option.

For those holding the purse strings, money may create significant push and pull factors for innovation too. Many system leaders in our study mentioned the creative freedom that additional ring-fenced finance gave them in the change process, as it enabled them to cover their start–up costs while still meeting existing statutory responsibilities. This is particularly important with radical innovations like Contextual Safeguarding, which are disruptive of existing systems. In the initial design and pilot of Contextual Safeguarding in Hackney, for example, the substantial funding received from the Children's Social Care Innovation Programme meant that the local authority could maintain its standard approach to child safeguarding for all children in the borough while it developed a parallel approach to addressing risks and harms in young people's peer groups and environments – which was particularly disruptive and expensive because it necessitated the introduction of entirely new information technology (IT) systems, multi-agency processes and practice tools (Lefevre et al, 2020).

Our interviews with expert informants in the first year of the Innovate Project, however, indicated that service leaders might be driven to try out a new practice method or system that is projected to be cheaper to deliver if they are unable to meet existing service responsibilities and outcome indicators within existing resources and capacity (Lefevre et al, forthcoming). It is important to note in such scenarios, however, that 'cheaper' does not necessarily mean 'cost-effective' (Suh and Holmes, 2022). A more expensive approach to service delivery might well offer value for money if it results in better outcomes for children and young people in the medium to longer term. Transitional Safeguarding, for example, has not tended to attract dedicated funding, yet cost savings across different systems and the human life course forms one of the major arguments for its inception (Holmes and Smale, 2018). Yet, if organisations and systems are unable to sustain new approaches within existing resources, they may not be viable to deliver in the longer term:

'The other thing is that innovation funding quite often is for one year, for two years, and there's a danger that, you know, you set up this great innovation project and then when the funding goes, you simply can't mainstream it because the money's not there. It's not because the will's not there, it's because you haven't got the money there across the whole system.' (Strategic service leader)

Hence, from inception, innovation planning should consider motivations for change, how and by whom aspired outcomes are to be judged, and the future sustainability of designs. These factors affect any subsequent analysis of whether innovation is the right way forward or whether more modest forms of continuous improvement (Keathley et al, 2013) or the better implementation of existing systems would be more appropriate (see Figure 2.2). Involving key stakeholders (for example, young people, parents, local communities and practitioners) in a meaningful way is as necessary as engaging those with experience of innovation design and implementation to lead or coordinate the introduction of a new approach (Sebba, 2017). The lived experiences of these stakeholders enhance both the practicality and trustworthiness of an innovation proposal (Hampson et al, 2021). Co-production processes can generate shared understandings of the nature of social problems, their potential solutions, the outcomes by which innovation success might be judged and the system capacity and capabilities that would be needed to achieve this. They can also lead to rich vision and shared commitment, which increases the strength and legitimacy of the case for change. In turn, this will be more persuasive in securing emotional and financial buy-in from key members of the 'authorising environment' (Moore, 2013), which includes senior managers, political leaders, commissioners and funders, and other local agency and community partners. Their support is crucial if any additional resourcing or strategic support is needed when the innovation experiences challenges along the way, as it invariably

Figure 2.2: Stage 1: mobilising for innovation

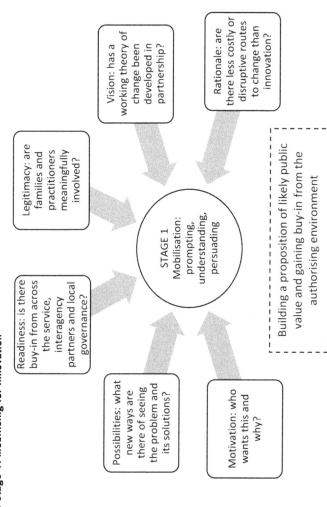

does. Indeed, as we found in our case-study sites, the lack of buy-in from strategic leaders was one of the biggest factors overall for those initiatives that struggled at various stages in their journey, even where there was strong and directional middle management in place.

Design and delivery in the local context

While our trajectory model of the six stages of innovation provides a directional map for the innovation journey, it is primarily indicative (representing phases, aims and considerations commonly seen within successful innovation practice) rather than prescriptive (a formula or manual for achieving success). Innovation is not a 'pipeline whereby ideas, resources, and the full range of prescribed activities [can] be fed in at one end, and aspired outcomes [will] flow out at the other' (Lefevre et al, 2022: 10). Rather, it is highly context dependent, affected by the domains and components set out in Figure 2.1. It is essential that the second – 'design' – stage of innovation (see Figure 2.3) begins with an audit of what capacity there already is in the system, including where there are sufficient numbers of people with the right sort of knowledge and skills, before specific aspects of design are considered. These factors will lie at the heart of the development of the 'theory of change' – a logic model that maps out how and why innovators think that a particular set of activities, design features and operational capabilities will result in identified goals being achieved within that specific context (Mulgan, 2019). It matters at both a practical and ethical level who generates the initial hypothesis for the theory of change and the process by which it is explored and concretised into a coherent plan. This is important because the problem that the innovation is intended to solve needs to be understood from the perspective of all those whom it most affects (Lankelly Chase Foundation, 2017).

The journey through the stages may not be unidirectional. As illustrated by developments in the Transitional Safeguarding

Figure 2.3: Stage 2: designing the innovation

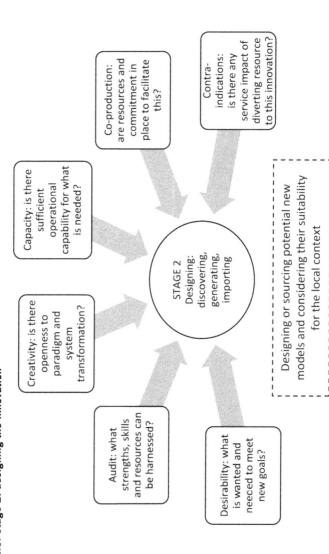

Co-production: are resources and commitment in place to facilitate this?

Contra-indications: is there any service impact of diverting resource to this innovation?

Capacity: is there sufficient operational capability for what is needed?

Creativity: is there openness to paradigm and system transformation?

STAGE 2 Designing: discovering, generating, importing

Audit: what strengths, skills and resources can be harnessed?

Desirability: what is wanted and needed to meet new goals?

Designing or sourcing potential new models and considering their suitability for the local context sites discussed in Chapter Three, an iterative revisiting of innovation phases is not uncommon and should perhaps even be expected, particularly between the stages of design and delivery, when new system features and tools are being piloted (see Figure 2.4). Relating this to the 'readiness' and operational capacity components set out in Figure 2.1, innovation processes may, and invariably do, take much longer than expected to reach full delivery and become embedded (Sebba et al, 2017; FitzSimons and McCracken, 2020).

This recursive, looping process will be particularly the case for entirely new innovations, as was the case with the Hackney pilot of Contextual Safeguarding, where, following Firmin's (2017) initial theorisation that the contexts of risk themselves needed to be addressed if extra-familial harms affecting young people were to be ameliorated, all system components, tools, procedures, relationships and practices needed to be envisaged from scratch. Some two years into the Hackney pilot, the theoretical refinement of the Contextual Safeguarding framework elaborated two levels at which systems needed to address extra-familial harm: (1) incorporating contextual thinking about extra-familial relationships, networks and locations into individual work with children and families; and (2) developing practices, systems and structures that identify, assess and intervene within the contexts in which harm occurs (Firmin and Lloyd, 2020).

Hackney had responded to this refinement by incorporating the first level into its standard children's social care offer while creating a specialist service of dedicated and highly skilled youth practitioners to encompass responsibilities at the second level. Stakeholders had hoped to have reached the integration stage of innovation after four years. However, when the second stage of evaluation was completed in the fifth year (Lefevre et al, 2023), this revealed that non-specialist staff in children's social care were not building up enough experience in working with situations of extra-familial harm to feel confident and skilled in building relationships with young

Figure 2.4: Stage 3: developing and piloting the innovation

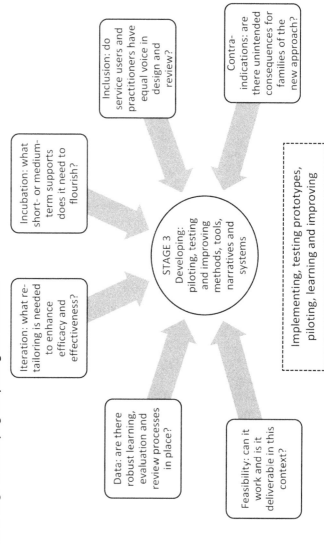

Iteration: what re-tailoring is needed to enhance efficacy and effectiveness?

Incubation: what short- or medium-term supports does it need to flourish?

Inclusion: do service users and practitioners have equal voice in design and review?

Contra-indications: are there unintended consequences for families of the new approach?

STAGE 3
Developing: piloting, testing and improving methods, tools, narratives and systems

Data: are there robust learning, evaluation and review processes in place?

Feasibility: can it work and is it deliverable in this context?

Implementing, testing prototypes, piloting, learning and improving

Figure 2.5: The iterative process of innovation as seen in the Hackney pilot

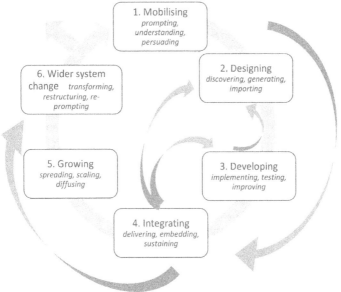

Source: Originally published in Lefevre et al (2023: 24)

people or addressing unsafe contexts, even though they were better able to recognise, assess and address risks with individual young people. The chosen design had, in fact, unexpectedly embedded a situation that sustained rather than addressed this skills disparity and that lacked long-term viability without additional ring-fenced resources.

As a result, Hackney needed to return to the design phase to fundamentally rethink the distribution of roles, tasks and responsibilities within children's services and at its interface with the interagency system (see Figure 2.5, originally published in Lefevre et al, 2023, p. 24). Our evaluation report concluded that 'this state of affairs does not reflect any lack of work or commitment on the part of Hackney'; rather, 'Given that the Contextual Safeguarding project constituted a highly ambitious programme of radical innovation, involving substantial iterative process change in systems, cultures and practices, then recursive loops of review and redesign should be expected, as with other transformative social innovations' (Lefevre et al, 2023: 92).

In the technology and human design industries, the mantra tends to be one of unharnessed creativity, where you 'fail often in order to succeed sooner'; such permissiveness allows innovators to generate and test new ideas rapidly on a small scale, focus energy on those that have potential to make an impact, and return iteratively to the design phase if initial attempts do not gain traction in practice (Zuber et al, 2005: 3). However, developing and piloting new initiatives in social care is complex and can be fraught with tension in these highly regulated and bureaucratised environments, where there is a high degree of staff churn, constraints on the public purse and pervasive anxieties about potential harm to very vulnerable children and young people within a wider culture of blame, shame and fear, often fuelled by hostile media reports or interventions by politicians (Brown and Osborne, 2013). This pressure is more likely to create a climate of risk aversion than creativity, and, in turn, as highlighted in Figure 2.1, this becomes a barrier to innovation processes. Staff often experience anxiety about getting innovations 'wrong', and managers worry that they might be wasting (or seen to be wasting) public money if they do not 'get it right' the first time (Laird et al, 2018). Chapter Five discusses what this anxiety looks like in practice and how it might be addressed.

It was notable in our fieldwork that case-study sites that were able to move readily back and forth between the design, delivery and embedding stages were those that felt more confident in the support of strategic leaders, the interagency network and local politicians when they needed to move in new directions or revise aspirations. Throughout piloting and improving innovations, leaders and managers need to create a climate of curiosity, flexibility, reflexivity and adaptability, in which anxiety is contained and learning through experience is enabled (Baldwin, 2008; McPheat and Butler, 2014; see also Chapter Six). Brown (2015) notes that the development of knowledge about how best to facilitate innovation is impeded by the relative avoidance in the social care sector of publishing accounts of when, why or how innovations have faltered, or have taken much longer than expected. This needs to change, as an enhanced understanding of what causes innovation to struggle, and how it might be scaffolded at pivotal moments, would help to challenge prevailing discourses about failure and success, and build a more conducive environment for innovation.

Integrating and sustaining innovation

Careful attention to implementation-specific issues is important throughout the innovation process but has particular pertinence at the point at which there are sustained efforts to embed a new approach into systems and routine practice (Fixsen et al, 2005). Even at its most basic, delivering a new approach is a complex multi-level task that can be beset with difficulties. This is true of any sector and in any country, but ensuring that a new approach is able to embed as 'business as usual' in social care can be a particular challenge given some of the typical complexities of welfare provision in countries dominated by neoliberal policies and discourses:

- bureaucratisation and high levels of regulation;
- preoccupation with, and anxieties about, risk;
- financial constraints amid a policy drive to reduce public spending;
- high staff turnover and shortages in a climate of accelerating demand;
- a requirement to engage with, and meet the demands of, multiple stakeholders, including many families with diverse characteristics and complex needs, some of whom are reluctant to engage or actively resist cooperation; and

- increased competition and the diversification of delivery in line with governmental aims of bringing new providers into the sector, alongside the push to deliver better outcomes (Brown and Osborne, 2012; Sebba, 2017; Jones, 2018; FitzSimons and McCracken, 2020; Jesus and Amaro, forthcoming; Van der Pas and Jansen, forthcoming).

However, while there has been significant investment in the design of innovations in social care, the sector does not routinely draw on implementation science or use evidence-based implementation tools (activities, models or frameworks) to support the change process (Aarons et al, 2011; Kaye et al, 2012). Not acknowledging the importance of implementation-related issues or a lack of planning and preparedness through the different stages of innovation increase the chances that an innovation will be poorly executed, that fidelity to the underpinning model is low, that desired outcomes will not be achieved and that the new approach will not embed and sustain (Aarons and Palinkas, 2007; Fixsen et al, 2009; Blase et al, 2012).

'Sustainability' can encompass financial viability, staff morale and energy, narrative momentum, and the ability of leaders to 'hold their nerve' during the period before outcomes improve and cost savings are realised. Services will need to put mechanisms in place that make the new approach part of the everyday pattern of practice while having the reflexive mindset that continually collects evidence, generates learning and adapts iteratively. This is challenging to achieve without losing the underpinning principles and values of the innovation, particularly given the ongoing threat of financial, political and staffing constraints. How to sustain an innovation as new staff join who have not been part of the original development process is a significant challenge. In some of our fieldwork sites, the need for an ongoing programme of training in new approaches and continuing attention to building and maintaining a culture that reflects the principles of the approaches had not been anticipated but became necessary due to staff turnover. Similarly, maintaining momentum and commitment when the key individuals that have championed, coordinated or directed the innovation have left the organisation can create significant risks. This was the case in three of our case-study sites, challenging progress at the point when our fieldwork was ending. We would suggest that the integration stage is where the viability of the innovation is truly tested. Succession planning needs to be in place from the start, so that vision, culture, enthusiasm and institutional knowledge do not rest with one or two key individuals without whom sustainability is jeopardised (see Figure 2.6).

Scaling, spreading and wider system change

Once an approach has been delivered successfully at a modest and local level, it might then be considered for trialling in different sites or scaling up across a larger area (see Figure 2.7). However, there remains an unresolved question as to whether scaling needs to be justified through clear evidence of impact on end-user outcomes (for example, the enhanced safety and well-being of young people) or whether promising smaller, short- to medium-term indicators, such as increased practitioner self-efficacy, efficient service operation and positive qualitative feedback from children, young people and families, are sufficient. Although innovation funding and evaluation expectations usually have short time frames (often one or two years, and very rarely over five), it can take a significant period, sometimes years, to produce the desired outcomes of innovation (Garcia et al, 2019). The typical time frame for an innovation to have significant impact at scale is much longer (Lankelly Chase Foundation, 2017). This adds further weight to arguments for trialling appropriately resourced, promising innovations at scale and at an early stage, as this will provide significantly more knowledge of

Figure 2.6: Stage 4: integrating the new approach as standard practice

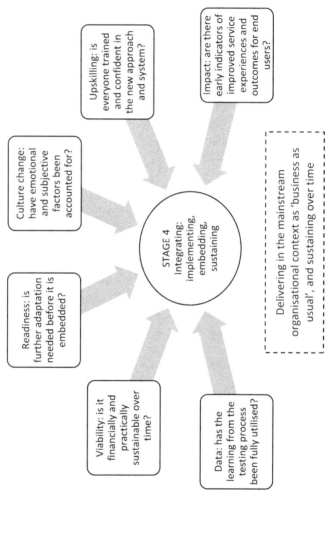

Readiness: is further adaptation needed before it is embedded?

Culture change: have emotional and subjective factors been accounted for?

Upskilling: is everyone trained and confident in the new approach and system?

Impact: are there early indicators of improved service experiences and outcomes for end users?

STAGE 4
Integrating: implementing, embedding, sustaining

Viability: is it financially and practically sustainable over time?

Data: has the learning from the testing process been fully utilised?

Delivering in the mainstream organisational context as 'business as usual', and sustaining over time

Figure 2.7: Stage 5: growing and spreading the innovation

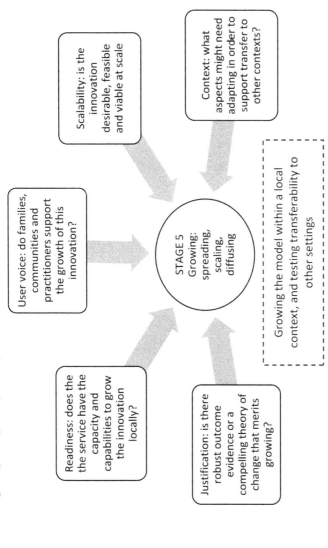

Scalability: is the innovation desirable, feasible and viable at scale

Context: what aspects might need adapting in order to support transfer to other contexts?

User voice: do families, communities and practitioners support the growth of this innovation?

STAGE 5
Growing:
spreading,
scaling,
diffusing

Growing the model within a local context, and testing transferability to other settings

Readiness: does the the service have the capacity and capabilities to grow the innovation locally?

Justification: is there robust outcome evidence or a compelling theory of change that merits growing?

the transferability and efficacy of an emergent approach across diverse contexts (Mulgan et al, 2007). Nonetheless, a note of caution should be sounded in relation to the risks of a programme that does not ultimately improve service experiences and outcomes for children and young people becoming embedded in wider systems.

Mulgan et al (2007) suggest that it is likely to take even longer, perhaps 10–15 years, before an initial idea reaches the point of being reflected in wider systemic change, for example, being incorporated into national policy and practice guidance (see Figure 2.8). This longer timescale is apparent in the three frameworks for practice and service innovation we considered through this project. Transitional Safeguarding was first coined as a term in 2018 (Holmes and Smale, 2018) and remains at a relatively early stage in its trajectory at the time of writing. Trauma-informed Practice was conceptualised in the US in 2001 but only started to appear in the UK children's social care sector from 2016. Since that time, it has infused a number of new approaches and is now reflected in Scottish policy through a practice toolkit (Scottish Government, 2021), as well as forming part of the principles of 'the Promise' made to children and families (The Promise, Scotland, 2020). However, as yet, it has not made any firm inroads into policy in the other countries of the UK.

Contextual Safeguarding has had the most rapid trajectory. The original doctoral research by Carlene Firmin that generated the initial ideas was conducted during 2011–15, and its theoretical formulation was published in 2016 (Firmin, 2017; Firmin et al, 2016). The framework received national funding for its first pilot (in Hackney) in 2017 and was being further trialled in nine test sites during 2019–21. By 2023, over 80 local authorities and third sector organisations had engaged with the framework in some form on the basis of its projected promise, and the approach was named within the national practice guidance for Scotland on tackling criminal exploitation with young people (Scottish Government, 2023).

Figure 2.8: Stage 6: transforming the wider system

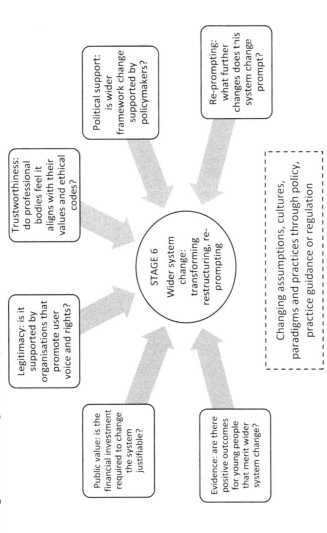

Trustworthiness: do professional bodies feel it aligns with their values and ethical codes?

Political support: is wider framework change supported by policymakers?

Re-prompting: what further changes does this system change prompt?

Legitimacy: is it supported by organisations that promote user voice and rights?

STAGE 6
Wider system change: transforming restructuring, re-prompting

Changing assumptions, cultures, paradigms and practices through policy, practice guidance or regulation

Public value: is the financial investment required to change the system justifiable?

Evidence: are there positive outcomes for young people that merit wider system change?

Yet, no firm evidence of impact outcomes on young people's safety is yet ascertainable (Lefevre et al, 2023).

Conclusion

This chapter has outlined system factors, dynamics and capabilities within each of the foundational contextual domains that need to be taken into account in the planning, implementation and review stages if they are to facilitate rather than impede innovation. The diagrams in this chapter provide key points to aid system audit and reflection at each stage. However, drawing on Costello and colleagues' (2011) integration of Bronfenbrenner's (2005) ecological systems theory with innovation practice, it can be seen that some factors and processes are more in the control of individuals than others. The personal competencies of practitioners and leaders are influenced by interpersonal relationships within the microsystems of teams and work with families. The operational capabilities, culture and climate of individual organisations (the 'mesosystem') are in dialogue with inter-organisational networks (the 'exosystem'). All practices and local policies are affected by the 'macrosystem' of law and public policy (Costello et al, 2011). Innovations aimed at whole-systems change are characterised by particular complexity and distributed power (see Chapter Three).

With respect to Contextual Safeguarding, the aspiration for addressing risks and harms across local and public environments in which young people live their lives can only be realised through interagency commitments at a practical as well as principled level. This requires far-reaching conversations at an early stage about underpinning theorisations of the nature of the problem that innovation is projected to address and about which agencies do, or should, hold responsibilities for particular roles and tasks. With respect to emergent issues, such as extra-familial risks and harms, some of these fundamental issues are not yet resolved. A key principle of Contextual

Safeguarding is that the social antecedents of harm must also be addressed; this requires a different approach at a political level to invest in the kind of public welfare measures and early intervention funding that ebbed away in the years of austerity (Billingham and Irwin-Rogers, 2022). While harms like child sexual exploitation have now been categorised within safeguarding procedures, there remains professional uncertainty about the degree to which the welfare needs of young people who are involved in 'crimes' like violence and criminal exploitation are prioritised over the prevention of crime and public protection (Lloyd et al, 2023). This can also not be fully resolved at a local level in countries, such as England, until the governance of child safeguarding, law enforcement and youth justice systems becomes better aligned within national systems (Firmin et al, 2022). As we go on to discuss further in Chapters Three and Four, it does often require a wider systemic take-up of an innovation before the promise that it offers can be truly operationalised.

Key chapter insights for policy and practice

- There are six stages common to innovation journeys in social care: (1) mobilising; (2) designing; (3) developing; (4) integrating; (5) growing; and (6) wider system change.
- The innovation journey is not necessarily linear, and stages are commonly revisited.
- Social care should draw more on implementation science and evidence-based implementation tools (activities, models or frameworks) to support the change process.
- Developing and piloting new initiatives in social care is complex and provokes anxiety because of the high level of vulnerability of service users.
- Risk aversion can be mediated where strategic leaders, the interagency network and local politicians create a supportive climate where curiosity, flexibility, reflexivity and adaptability are enabled.
- Innovation may be motivated by a hope that it will enable existing service responsibilities and outcome indicators to be met within

existing resources. However, 'cheaper' does not necessarily mean 'value for money'.
- More accounts are needed of innovations that struggle, as this will build understanding of how to scaffold innovation at pivotal moments.

THREE

Recursiveness in early-stage innovation

Introduction

In this chapter, we examine early-stage innovation in the field of extra-familial risks and harms through the lens of Transitional Safeguarding, a framework that envisions 'whole-systems' change. As outlined in Chapter One, Transitional Safeguarding is not a prescribed model; rather, it invites innovation based on local needs and the collaboration of a diverse array of local partners, including young people and their communities. While this allows for flexibility and co-production, it can also add particular complexity to innovation projects. We discuss some of the challenges, opportunities and key themes that have emerged for local areas seeking to create more 'transitionally attuned' local safeguarding systems. In addition to the insights generated by extensive ethnographic work in our two Transitional Safeguarding case-study sites, the chapter also draws on key informant interviews, reflective discussion groups and journey-mapping interviews with a number of other local areas in our wider community of practice that were also in the process of introducing Transitional Safeguarding.

In our analysis, we argue that the principles of complexity theory and the ecocycles model of development (Holling, 1987; Hurst and Zimmermann, 1994; Lipmanowicz and

McCandless, 2013) provide a useful perspective for considering the experiences of our research sites during their early paths of Transitional Safeguarding innovation journeys, as they allow us to consider the decentralised, emergent, iterative and recursive character of change processes, situating them within a long-term view rather than judging them as either 'successes' or 'failures'.

The complexity of whole-systems change

Transitional Safeguarding as a boundary-spanning concept

As outlined in Chapter One, Transitional Safeguarding envisions whole-systems change that is locally configured and involves co-production among a variety of organisations and services across sectors (for example, social care, health, education, housing, youth and criminal justice, and the voluntary sector), and with young people and their communities. 'Transitional' refers not only to how young people should be supported into adulthood but also to the need for safeguarding systems to span boundaries between – often siloed – services and systems (Holmes, 2022). A key informant in our research, involved in conceptualising Transitional Safeguarding principles at national levels, outlined how this means that change cannot be limited to parts of a system:

'It will not work if just one sector responds. So, if you have an initiative that's based in children's services and doesn't involve adult services' colleagues right the way through, it will not work … there's no one right way of doing it because every local authority is different. It has different priorities, it has different populations, and they will know their populations best. … Transitional Safeguarding can be a little bit difficult to grasp because there's not a, "Well, do this and it's going to get sorted". It's not that straightforward.' (Key informant)

The complexity of Transitional Safeguarding innovation is linked to its central premise of holism: it is not limited to new services for young adults, to extending existing services for children into early adulthood or to increasing the activities of statutory adult social care services to better respond to extra-familial risks and harms. All these aspects may be part of the 'whole-system, whole-person, whole-place wellbeing' transformation (Holmes and Bowyer, 2020) that Transitional Safeguarding seeks to achieve, but they are unlikely to solve issues in isolation.

Current societal challenges wrought by years of public sector austerity, the COVID-19 pandemic and a landscape of political and economic uncertainty in the UK provide a challenging backdrop for Transitional Safeguarding. Among the plethora of issues affecting both children's and adult social care services in these contexts, questions about whether there is enough political will and momentum to prioritise creating better support and safeguarding systems for young people (see Chapter Five) are particularly live for Transitional Safeguarding. Unlike some other innovations focused on services for children (Department for Education, 2022), to date, Transitional Safeguarding has not attracted any dedicated funding from government sources. These challenges, along with the potentially overwhelming magnitude of the envisioned change, lend further weight to considering early endeavours to adopt the concept through a complexity perspective.

A complexity theory lens

Complexity is a key feature of the risks and harms experienced by young people, and therefore also needs to be a characteristic of responses to these problems (Firmin et al, 2022; Huegler and Ruch, 2022). Recent years have seen calls for public service and systems development to embrace key principles of complexity theory (see, for example, Fish and Hardy, 2015; Rutter et al, 2017; Lowe and French, 2021). Complexity theory focuses on interactions between parts of complex adaptive systems, particularly where these parts are characterised by dispersed and distributed control and power, non-linearity, and unpredictability. Having emerged from a range of fields and disciplines, complexity theory is transdisciplinary and blends diverse ideas and approaches (Gear et al, 2018).

In the context of 'whole-system change' innovations like Transitional Safeguarding, the principles of complexity theory offer a focus on the dynamic interactions between diverse and distributed agents and processes, with outcomes being hard or impossible to predict. Individual organisations responding to young people affected by extra-familial risks and harms, the local area ecology of such responses, and the national social policy landscapes directing such work are all examples of complex adaptive systems at different scales that operate in interaction (Lowe and French, 2021). The ways in which adaptive development (and hence innovation) happens in these systems involves recursive processes, that is, successive and interdependent iterations, whereby even small changes in practices can have significant repercussions. Processes of adaptation may include emergent and spontaneous self-organisation, such as the forming of informal groups or alliances that circumvent existing boundaries or hierarchies to promote the proliferation of new ideas. Boundaries in complex systems are socially constructed rather than objectively 'given'; they connect rather than separate system contexts (Gear et al, 2018). Hence, the boundary spanning of Transitional Safeguarding innovation involves, above all, connection, networking, building and sustaining relationships through processes that can be described as examples of human learning systems (Lowe and French, 2021; see also Chapter Seven).

Our learning about Transitional Safeguarding innovation reveals themes of unpredictable emergence, diverse and distributed power, constructed boundaries as sites of connection, and iterative learning loops. In the following sections, we will use the perspective of recursive 'ecocycles' to outline how these processes influence early-stage innovation journeys involving and aiming for 'whole-system' change.

An ecocycles perspective

Innovation processes in social care have been described as following cyclical development phases that are not necessarily linear, from the conception of ideas and early exploration through to propagation and, eventually, spreading to systemic change (Hartley, 2006; Mulgan et al, 2007; Murray et al, 2010; Lefevre et al, 2022; see also Chapter Two). Not all stages may be experienced by every innovation endeavour. In this chapter, we turn to a perspective that extends this cyclical model to include the role of recursiveness and feedback loops that characterise change in complex adaptive systems. The idea of 'ecocycles' is represented as extending from a circle to an intertwined 'infinity' loop symbol. First proposed by Holling (1987) as symbolising four key functions and phases of a complex ecosystem, it was applied by Hurst and Zimmerman (1994) to the complex processes characterising human organisations and their connected environments. The four phases (see Figure 3.1) range through the following processes: (1) the emergence and 'exploitation' (effective use) of available resources for growth; (2) consolidation and maturation; (3) 'creative destruction' (which may involve actions, inaction or contextual 'forces'); and (4) renewal, where resources are once again mobilised for a further iteration of the ecocycle. The back loop of creative destruction and renewal does not mean a return to the exact same starting point; instead, it 'places complex systems in a cycle of continual transformation' (Hurst and Zimmerman, 1994: 341).

The ecocycles model has become a feature of organisational and project planning, having been popularised by its inclusion as one of 33 'liberating structures' (Lipmanowicz and McCandless, 2013), a repertoire of micro-approaches designed to promote collaborative and co-produced innovation processes. In this chapter, we use the ecocycles lens to trace and map four key phases in the early stages of Transitional Safeguarding development often observed within our case-study sites:

Figure 3.1: Adaptation of the ecocycles model

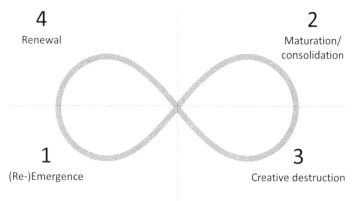

4 Renewal

2 Maturation/consolidation

1 (Re-)Emergence

3 Creative destruction

Source: Adapted from Hurst and Zimmermann (1994), Holling (1987) and Lipmanowicz and McCandless (2013)

1. The taking up of Transitional Safeguarding ideas as a phase of (re-)emergence, drawing on previous ideas or initiatives where local innovation leads (whether in formal leadership positions or not) proposed a case for change. Enthusiasm and energy often characterised this phase.
2. The establishment of initial, and sometimes temporary, practices aimed at connecting professionals from different agencies (through working groups, panels, boards, protocols or hubs) and, in some cases, directly involving young people and community organisations. These practices generated and surfaced productive struggles and debates around the scope, directions and moral imperatives of required change. Such groups and practices were generally perceived not to be the 'end point' of Transitional Safeguarding development but rather as milestones on a longer-term journey.
3. A sense, at times, of stasis, impasse or even of decline and 'failure', when the potential for systems change was most likely to be questioned.
4. Anticipation of, hopefulness about and some indications of renewal, often accompanied by a resigned conviction that

the persistence of the issues that Transitional Safeguarding seeks to address would lead to a return to this work at some point in the future.

We will now consider key features of these processes in turn.

Emergence of innovation ideas and making the case for change

Recursiveness is embedded in the very foundation of Transitional Safeguarding, as it both connects with long-standing concerns about the lacking capacity of systems to support young people during transition to adulthood and, concurrently, proposes new ways of framing these issues through the lens of safeguarding. For example, concerns about transitional support for young adults with complex needs (Social Exclusion Unit, 2005) or in the criminal justice system (Barrow Cadbury Commission, 2005) had been raised from the early 2000s. Similarly, our research partners spoke of the concept as naming "something that previously wasn't named" and referred to examples of "unusual allies … who are doing Transitional Safeguarding, actually, without calling it 'Transitional Safeguarding'" (innovation lead). Thus, the taking up of Transitional Safeguarding ideas and the decision to embark on innovation in line with this concept represented not just a phase of emergence of new ideas but also a degree of reconnecting with previous ideas and initiatives. Examples in our case-study sites prior to 'Transitional Safeguarding' being coined as a term included transitions projects or transitions worker posts in areas with large-scale police-led operations (linked to heightened public awareness) in response to the sexual exploitation of children and vulnerable adults. However, public attention shifting away from these issues had made such initiatives vulnerable to being de-prioritised, manifesting in decreased funding or 'dormant' unfilled posts.

The launching of Transitional Safeguarding initiatives created a sense of momentum about possibilities for change. During this phase of (re-)emergence, we noted in our sites evidence of both enthusiasm and ambivalence about the possibility of systems change, paired with a recognition that significant energy was needed in the context of 'change fatigue' in public services:

'It's about that kind of enthusiasm and energy because … in public services, especially now in the pandemic, you know, people are tired, and people are fed up of instability, and people are fed up of change, and so you've got to be really careful about how you approach a change.' (Innovation lead)

In one site, again, prior to 'Transitional Safeguarding' having been coined as a term, work to create more transitionally attuned structures had been prompted by a crisis associated with a large-scale police investigation and subsequent public reports into the sexual exploitation of young people under and over 18. This led to the establishment of a dedicated transitional service. At the time, the energy of this change felt "like a rocket": "everybody was driving it; everybody wanted it to work; everybody was on the same page" (service manager). Such energy and commitment, while marking enthusiasm for opportunities to effect change, also spoke to the pressures felt by professionals to mitigate the catastrophic consequences that extra-familial risks and harms can have in the lives of young people. In Chapter Five, we explore how such pressures can impact our expectations of what innovations might achieve.

Maturing and consolidating innovation plans and efforts

The initial commitment to innovation was often followed by periods of intensive work by the innovation leads in our various sites to rally support from different parts of local systems. Only in a minority of cases did this involve access to dedicated time or posts. Some areas actively involved young people and grass-roots community organisations, seeking their views on the most pressing issues. This phase of "listening to what young people are saying around what their risks and fears are" (innovation lead) was key for informing work plans and proposals, reflecting the centrality of participative principles within the Transitional Safeguarding concept.

However, these processes of co-production can also involve some tensions and challenges to professional perspectives, notably, that issues young people and grass-roots organisations identify as priorities do not necessarily overlap with what professionals consider to be urgent safeguarding risks. This is particularly relevant in a context that involves the reframing of safeguarding concepts to make them more expansive, inclusive and attentive to structural harms, as Transitional Safeguarding and Contextual Safeguarding have proposed, respectively (Holmes, 2022; Wroe, 2022). Balancing the widening of definitions with maintaining a focus on the acute risks facing young people in the highest situational vulnerability was a central theme for the conceptual work undertaken by sites during this phase:

'It feels like we've got a very broad approach thinking about need, risk and harm, so there's quite a bit of work around … transitional needs for young adults. So, some of the actions that have come forward have been based on what young people have said … 'I need to know what services are available to me. Who's going to help me with my housing? Who's going to help me with benefits? Who's going to help me with my mental health needs?'… [This] is really important but … how do we make sure we retain a focus on Transitional Safeguarding for those young adults at the most acute risk of harm, i.e., death, rape, etc, and not just think about generic needs across the board?' (Head of service)

Debates and "misconception about what Transitional Safeguarding is and what we're trying to achieve" (innovation lead) were also live in other areas, where workshops and conversations between hitherto disconnected and siloed services and organisations constituted a key part of the Transitional Safeguarding development work:

> 'I spent a lot of time explaining to people … this is about system innovation and … supporting young people throughout adulthood and adolescent development … this is about working beyond eligibility. And I think, for our commissioning board, that's something that was really hard for them to grasp. They couldn't understand why we would want to do that because, for them … they were like, "Well, we're already achieving it for these people, and the people that you're talking about now, they clearly just, they don't have need" … they're still very diagnosis led.' (Innovation lead)

Similarly, in another site, the productive struggles of this phase of work focused on convincing leaders in adult services to realise that existing services were not meeting the needs of young people affected by extra-familial risks and harms. Several individuals leading the introduction of a new system or approach in our research relied on being resourceful and working through relationships rather than strictly adhering to hierarchical structures of communication. In one example, a local area project manager used an interim report from the research team to convince senior leaders in a meeting of the need to address system gaps, describing the result as "push and awakening".

In the context of the various challenges and struggles that influence the 'ruling relations' of innovation practice (Smith, 2005: 51), such as austerity, professional fatigue in the wake of the COVID-19 pandemic and local crises (see Chapter Five), professionals often focused on the moral purpose and significance of Transitional Safeguarding as "the right thing to do" (innovation lead). In particular, the drive to introduce Transitional Safeguarding was the concern that, without change, young people might come to serious harm, even die (see also Preston-Shoot et al, 2022). Reconciling such moral imperatives with the often slow pace of change in social care demands flexibility, persistence and the tolerance of uncertainty. In one site that had been developing transitionally attuned practice over several years, a service manager outlined the challenges of these balancing acts: in direct work with young people, small "baby steps" of change are often expected and accepted by practitioners, and may even lead to strengthened resolve about the importance of this work. However, where practitioners are confronted with the inflexibility of systems and their seemingly unyielding resistance to change, particularly as part of endeavours to innovate for systems change, this seems much harder to accept or tolerate: "If you're passionate, and you want it to work and do well, and things aren't working, the system is … that's what starts burning you out. It's not the people I've supported, the service user or the family that burns you out; it's the systems" (service manager).

This interplay between hope and pessimism, described as sometimes amounting to "emotional oscillation" (innovation lead), speaks to the deeply personal impact of this work that we noted across the sites and the heaviness of the task that innovation 'leaders' have to bear (see Chapter Five). Where those leading innovation projects are close to practice rather than in strategic positions of authority and power, the need for support and emotionally containing spaces during the challenging, long-term and endurance-demanding efforts to change whole systems and structures is particularly strong. In Chapter Six, we consider how these demands in processes of change may lead to defences at organisational levels, undermining their capacity for transforming systems and practices. Such factors play no small part in the vulnerability of early-stage innovation projects to being derailed.

Declining momentum

Transitional Safeguarding developments in our fieldwork represent examples of early-stage innovation. For some sites embarking on the innovation journey, despite early challenges, progress and overall outlooks were promising: "We're still on the journey of those conversations … we're at a position with Transitional Safeguarding where, at board level, we've got that ownership and that agreement to the concept, which I think's quite amazing really" (senior leader). However, in other areas, initial energy and widespread support for the idea of Transitional Safeguarding had been overshadowed by challenges that sometimes seemed insurmountable. The most common ones concerned absent or declining leadership support, changes in staff or priorities among senior leaders, waning support and participation from specific parts of a local system, and a loss of additional resources or funding to support initial work.

Worsened conditions and contexts of work had a significant emotional impact, with expressions during meetings and interviews invoking both notions of fighting and a degree of mourning: "a constant battle, a constant challenge … [which feels] like it's gone backwards a little bit because compassion fatigue, impact on resources, cost of living, austerity. … I feel like there's less and less people with that same passion and drive around it" (service manager). In such contexts, even work perceived as very meaningful and successful can seem to be 'dwindling' or feel 'a failure'. Debates around the role of 'failure' are common in the overall innovation literature but a less openly discussed subject in social care innovations (Brown, 2015). Conversely, the history of children's social care in England is overshadowed by narratives of failure. From a linear perspective, 'failure' might seem to mark the end of interest in, and engagement with, an idea, increasing the stakes and pressures on professionals to perform success (see Chapter Five).

Difficulties were compounded in areas where one or two people were left 'in charge' of endeavours for whole-systems change without sufficient support:

'It's mad that you all think there's only one person that has got this … and without that ownership of our project group, and without people wanting to come to meetings and all that kind of stuff, absolutely you will lose traction, and it won't be because it's been deliberate; it will be because … you're all focused on other things, whilst coming and saying warm words.' (Innovation lead)

'I can't really think of the project as anything else but a failure. And I know that's maybe a bit harsh, but … in my head, I don't look back at that project and think, "Wow, we've really achieved something fantastic here". It just feels like it's kind of failed and it hasn't achieved anywhere close to what I would hope it would when we were initially doing the project. … It's not failing because of my lack of attempting to do that; it's failing because my, the lack of support that I'm being given by people who should really be giving support.' (Innovation lead)

While staff changes, particularly in the middle ranks of local authority leadership, are not uncommon, in two local areas, these pressures led to the professionals tasked with 'leading on' Transitional Safeguarding innovation – without themselves being in a position in the systemic hierarchy to direct or decree change – leaving their posts after instrumental periods of dedicated work. Despite the achievements of their work, which included involving young people and substantial groundwork to boost the case for change in their local areas, at the point of leaving, feelings of frustration, disappointment and a sense of failure dominated.

Renewing momentum

In our research, we found that even those professionals who spoke of feelings of failure or of having been failed by unsupportive cultures or structures did not consider this the end of Transitional Safeguarding developments in their local areas overall. Above all, this was grounded in their conviction that the principles of Transitional Safeguarding remained ethically, morally and practically justified in response to long-standing and persisting issues: "These problems won't … haven't gone away; they've been there for a long, long time. And do I feel confident they will have gone away in two years' time, five years' time? No, not really" (innovation lead). It was also clear that professionals were realistic about being "in … for the long haul" and "about what's achievable and how long it's going to take" (innovation lead). In one area, an innovation project lead considered that the recognition that "this isn't going away" could actually lend weight to an innovation endeavour, as the recurrence of issues served as a reminder that inaction "isn't an option" (innovation lead). For some, a long-term view provided a sense of hopefulness that, one day in the future, this work would regain priority status and their present efforts would pave the way for a smoother and more informed further iteration:

> 'I feel like it's going to be one of those things that, like, you know, when something gets put in a time capsule, and you think like everyone's going to absolutely forget about this in two minutes, and then maybe sometime, somewhere, people will realise they're going to do it, and I've already done all this work, and they don't need to do it again! … And they could maybe take the ideas and run with them.' (Innovation lead)

In policy and practice contexts where short funding and development cycles, as well as high staff turnover, are becoming increasingly commonplace, there are important questions about how learning and achievements across successive loops of innovation can be preserved. In particular, those involved in co-producing and leading innovations may need to consider how organisations, communities and individuals might be enabled to become collective 'memory holders' of such learning. We discuss the role of learning partnerships in innovation in more detail in Chapter Seven.

Conclusion

This chapter has considered some of the dynamics that may occur in early-stage innovation in social care through the lens of our case-study research on Transitional Safeguarding – an emergent framework aimed at whole-systems change. The complexity and potential scale of the transformation implied by the framework, and the absence of fixed models or blueprints for change, require flexibility, patience and persistence from those involved in this work. Using principles of complexity theory and the ecocycles model of systems development and innovation processes, we propose that the experiences of early-stage Transitional Safeguarding development journeys can be considered through a perspective of multidimensional and recursive 'ecocycle' loops. Importantly, and as outlined in Figure 3.2, we propose that the loops of different iterations do not (usually) return to the same starting point; rather, each time, the work undertaken influences and enriches the next version of innovation. Similarly, and as outlined by Lefevre et al (2022), this is not a deterministic model: developments may skip a phase or spin off to further refining work or in different directions altogether.

The ecocycles perspective (and, with it, the question of how collective memories of previous iterations can be preserved) also draws attention to the significance of innovation as, above all, a practice connected to human learning (Lowe and French, 2021; see also Chapter Seven). This is particularly relevant in a social policy landscape marred both by short-termism and the long-term hollowing-out effects of austerity. Hence, while innovation aimed at whole-systems change should be built on ideas of change that are disruptive, it is also important to recognise the need for emotional containment for leaders and practitioners alike, and for the continuity of relationships and learning within these processes (see Chapters Six and Seven).

Figure 3.2: Multidimensional recursive loops in early-stage innovation

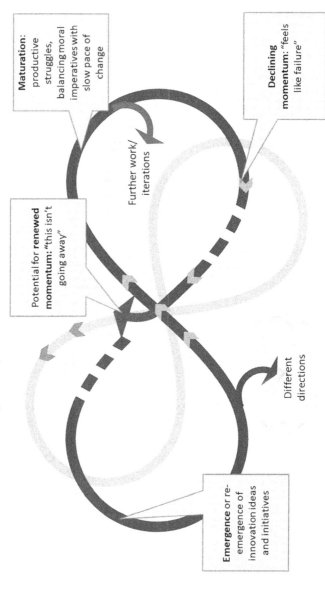

Maturation: productive struggles, balancing moral imperatives with slow pace of change

Declining momentum: "feels like failure"

Further work/ iterations

Potential for **renewed momentum:** "this isn't going away"

Different directions

Emergence or re-emergence of innovation ideas and initiatives

Key chapter insights for policy and practice

- Innovations that aim to transform and change whole systems through participative and co-productive processes, involving a diverse range of actors, are characterised by a complexity that makes their development journeys hard to predict or control centrally.
- The early stages of such innovations may be characterised by iterative loops of activity and learning, where momentum may fluctuate and include potential phases of decline and reinvigoration.
- The 'ecocycles' perspective offers a helpful lens for understanding the dynamics that may be at play in these phases.
- While co-produced innovations may offer the potential for transformational and enduring change to create better systems and services, they also pose particular challenges for those in charge of leading or facilitating projects and initiatives.
- This means that (collective) consideration needs to be given to how those involved in innovation endeavours can be appropriately supported and how learning across cycles can be sustained and preserved.

FOUR

Deciding between innovation and practice improvement measures

Introduction

What counts as innovation is up for debate and is explored in various ways in this book. As we set out in Chapter One, commonly used definitions of innovation imply new designs, systems and interventions that go some way beyond improvement of existing approaches towards more radically different ways of thinking and acting than those generally found within conventional service structures and paradigms (Murray et al, 2010; Young Foundation, 2012; Nesta, 2016; OECD and Eurostat, 2018). A key point of discussion that this definition gave rise to within our fieldwork was whether new approaches that seek to improve local practices but without disrupting local systems should be classified as 'innovative' practice improvement measures or if they constituted actual 'innovation'. In this chapter, we consider whether distinctions between the two terms might be more porous than the literature sometimes suggests. We illustrate key points through examples from two case-study sites in our research that were seeking to implement Trauma-informed Practice and where we noted both facets of incremental service improvement and whole-system innovation. In this chapter, we refer to the two organisations as Sites A and B. Site A remained on a journey of service improvement throughout our fieldwork, while Site B, latterly, additionally engaged in innovation-oriented transformation.

Considerations in introducing Trauma-informed Practice

As described in Chapter One, Trauma-informed Practice offers a strengths-based way of working that prioritises physical, emotional and relational safety, seeks to avoid re-traumatising service users, and works collaboratively with service users to enable them to regain control and autonomy (Harris and Fallot, 2001). While the framework was first evolved to improve individual practice with those who had experienced trauma, including developmental trauma through childhood abuse and neglect, the importance of supporting and protecting workers from the potential effects of what has been variously called 'vicarious trauma', 'compassion fatigue' or 'secondary traumatic stress' has also been recognised (Méndez-Fernández et al, 2022). While some literature has focused on individual practitioners' personal resilience, there has been an increasing interest in the role that employers might need to play not only in enabling workers to remain healthy and effective in their work but also in creating the organisational conditions that would enable practice to be reliably trauma informed (Hickle, 2019). It will be useful at this point for readers to refer back to Box 1.1 in Chapter One, which sets out key features of Trauma-informed Practice in the context of young people affected by extra-familial risks and harms. The outline provided there highlights how practitioners require care, support and supervisory processes from their organisations that are very similar to those that young people and other traumatised service users need from their workers (Sweeney et al, 2016; Hickle, 2019; Hickle and Lefevre, 2022).

Comparing innovation and 'continuous improvement'

As noted in Chapter One, rather than offering a model to be implemented with fidelity, the framework of principles associated with Trauma-informed Practice needs to be interpreted and tailored to each specific context and set of delivery aims. This necessity encouraged both sites to frame their aspirations for introducing Trauma-informed Practice as innovation. Yet, as became clear, each had (initially at least) a change process in mind that involved layering new ways of thinking and doing into the existing service over time rather than overturning how existing work was delivered. Their envisaged process of interpolated improvements to service delivery exemplified to us the rather loose way in which the concept of innovation is understood in the UK social care sector (Hampson et al, 2021).

The standard social innovation model that social care draws upon entails either creating something entirely new (invention) or transferring a promising model or practice from a different context or discipline and tailoring it to a local context or need with some degree of fidelity to the original model (adaptation) (Murray et al, 2010). While there is no expectation that innovation, in its broadest sense, is values driven, both 'continuous improvement' (Keathley et al, 2013) and social innovation seek to create positive value. In the case of social innovation, this is through broad aspirations to create a positive impact on individuals and improve the societal structures that lead to better outcomes for all. For practice improvement measures, it is through more instrumental attempts to improve public services in ways that are intended to improve experiences and outcomes for target groups or achieve service efficiencies (Bason, 2018).

A key distinction between the two is the ground-breaking or transformative nature of innovation and its explicit (often radical) discontinuity with the past. For those working in social care, the term 'innovation' can elicit strong positive and negative emotions, and often both at the same time. Innovation can mean opportunity, possibility, creativity, a leap of faith into the world we want and the ability to grow green shoots of change in difficult circumstances; however, it is also hard work, provokes anxiety and uncertainty, and can cause painful disruption and destruction of tried-and-tested structures (Murray et al, 2010; Young Foundation, 2012; Mulgan, 2019). Innovation may not create immediate solutions to service challenges and so may feel like a needless rocking of the boat on the stormy seas of a cash-strapped, regulation-heavy social care sector, particularly where a team or organisation is labouring in the wake of a critical service inspection or a practice review following the death or serious abuse of a vulnerable child or adult.

Continuous improvement, in contrast, is commonly iterative, methodical and incremental, with each (often small) cycle of change building on the former once it appears beneficial and stable (Brown and Osborne, 2012). The aim is to optimise existing approaches, enhance quality, efficiency or cost-effectiveness in established systems and practices, and eliminate deficiencies (Keathley et al, 2013). While it could also achieve the transformation of service structures and outcomes, this would be achieved through 'a steady stream of improvements, diligently executed' (Dewar et al, 2019). In these ways, improvement-directed processes may feel more practical and achievable than innovation, as they build on existing knowledge and resources (Accept Mission, 2023). Maintaining 'business as usual' without disruption is a key consideration, particularly where there are statutory obligations to support vulnerable individuals. A concurrency approach may enable improvements in current provision to be continued and built upon while new approaches are being tested (Mulgan, 2014).

As we noted in our earlier evidence review of promising and effective professional responses to extra-familial risks and harms (Firmin et al, 2022), an important early decision for services considering whether and how to change is whether aims for increased efficiency and effectiveness can be achieved through the improvement of existing services or whether a more fundamental rethinking of paradigms and systems (innovation) is required. A key consideration as to whether incremental improvement might be sufficient is whether the local context (infrastructure, governance and operational capabilities) and wider systems (policy, practice guidance, funding mechanisms and regulatory processes) already provide enablement within the foundational contextual domains (see Chapter Two), which a particular approach needs to mobilise, gain traction and flourish.

Trauma-informed Practice, as noted earlier, is rooted in the establishment of trusting, collaborative relationships that help build safe psychological spaces for young people and practitioners alike (Hickle, 2019). As practitioners' own skills, personal qualities and emotional capacity are pivotal within this, such 'use of self' requires a scaffolding system structure without which (arguably) Trauma-informed Practice cannot fully be operationalised and thrive. First, the systems need to provide manageable caseloads and more flexible timescales for intervention, so that there is time for practitioners to get to know young people in a relaxed way, build trust and be there when the young person is ready to engage (Lefevre et al, 2017). Second, services need to provide the kind of reflective, emotionally 'containing' supervision and work context (Ruch, 2020: 5) that enables practitioners to process and make meaning of (mentalise) young people's experience, behaviour and non-verbal communications, and respond in empathically attuned ways. These two considerations are not only associated with more effective practice and improved outcomes for young people; they also mediate the possible risks of vicarious trauma for practitioners who are needing to engage at a deep level with young people who have experienced serious levels of abuse and trauma (Hickle and Lefevre, 2022). As we move forward now to consider what was observed in two of our case-study sites, the key question raised by our earlier evidence review has particular pertinence: 'Would a better implementation of existing guidance and intervention models enable professionals to spend the time needed to build relationships with the young people they support, or is the only way to achieve this to disrupt the current status quo and redesign the system from scratch?' (Firmin et al, 2022: 90–1).

Features of improvement-led approaches in both sites

The two case-study sites (A and B) seeking to introduce Trauma-informed Practice across their services were each responsible for the delivery of statutory children's social care services in their local area of the UK. Neither had a service focus specifically and solely on extra-familial risks and harms; practice with young people affected by safeguarding risks beyond the home was generally carried out by social workers who might be either in short-term assessment and intervention roles or within teams focused on longer-term work, including with young people in or leaving care.

Ethnographic fieldwork was conducted in three separate time periods of approximately four months across a two-year period. In the first time period, both sites seemed to be of a similar mind in viewing Trauma-informed Practice as a useful addition to existing approaches, particularly in respect of its potential capacity to enable a better understanding of the impact of developmental trauma on a young person's needs and functioning, and on young people's capacity to assess risk and form safe and healthy relationships. In essence, the organisations intended to continue to deliver the same overall service but to do so 'better', rather than seeking to question the underpinning ethos of their approach with young people affected by extra-familial risks and harms or making any fundamental transformations to existing systems or methods.

The delivery across the service of a targeted training programme was seen by both sites as the key early-stage route to the introduction of Trauma-informed Practice. The take-up and impact of practitioner training were the main indicators of the progression of the implementation. The effect of the training on staff was measured through participant feedback regarding the degree to which workers now understood the new approach and felt confident in using their new learning within their practice. In this sense, increased practitioner awareness and self-efficacy were equated by the sites with successful implementation. However, there was little hard evidence as to if, or how, what had been learned during the training had been translated into specific trauma-informed practices with young people. In part, this may have been because of the limited way in which training effectiveness was being measured; methods like service-user feedback or observational data regarding changes to practice, which tend to be more reliable than worker self-report, were not included (Pecukonis et al, 2016). Moreover, while practitioners generally described finding the training helpful, the feedback gathered from practice supervisors on what they perceived the impact of the training to be, revealed uncertainty as to whether their staff were working differently or in line with the principles of the new framework.

Exploring this further with senior leaders during interviews, and examining documentation from the sites, it emerged that there was much less clarity across each site about the mechanisms by which the trauma-informed awareness developed during training was hypothesised to lead to better practice. Leaders had assumed that once training had been delivered, the new learning would sustain over time for those individuals. However, this is not a supposition that can be relied upon, as other studies of the complex relationship between skills and outcomes, and the challenges of transforming practice in children's services, have found (Forrester et al, 2018). For new learning to become embedded as practice as usual for all staff, and for this to sustain beyond the frequent turnover of staff in public services, other changes are also needed in the practice system, such as incorporating the new approach into supervisory practices (Pecukonis et al, 2016).

This emphasis on enabling workers to think differently about young people, rather than on what either individuals or the service as a whole might need to do differently, was part of a 'low-cost' and 'low-demand' paradigm of change. The senior leaders in both sites were aware of how overstretched staff in these statutory services already were, and there was a reluctance to add to existing burdens, as this could be counterproductive:

'Colleagues in social care are really struggling at the moment: there's been budget cuts; there's been reductions in staff numbers; we've got huge caseloads; people are overwhelmed. And I think that will mean we have to tread very, very carefully because what we don't want to do is be coming in at colleagues and saying, "Look, you are really overwhelmed at the moment and we recognise that, but here's a load of extra stuff we want you to do. ... We want you to relearn how to do assessments; we want you to change all the paperwork that you're used to using; we want all of this". And my fear is that if it's not managed very, very carefully, rather than embedding a trauma-informed approach within the workforce, we actually lose some of our workforce.' (Site A, senior leader)

By framing Trauma-informed Practice as something that did not require more fundamental service reforms, just the same work practised or viewed differently, it could be seen by these sites as a low-cost means of practice improvement. This was particularly the case in Site A, where ring-fenced funding to implement Trauma-informed Practice beyond the start-up costs of its initial trial period was not available. Given other pressing commitments in that site and external funding constraints, senior leaders were forced to decide that the ongoing rollout and sustaining of the new approach needed to be subsumed within existing structures. They could see no feasible alternative to this, other than dropping the approach altogether and letting any progress made just ebb away. This was a significant moment for Site A, as the lack of resources to change systems at a more fundamental level severely limited the possibilities for realising the innovative affordances of Trauma-informed Practice.

It was at this point that the approaches taken by Sites A and B to introducing Trauma-informed Practice started to diverge. Site B was also struggling with the time-poor and cash-strapped nature of children's services:

> '[Site name]'s up against it, as every other council is as well. We don't have a big enough workforce because I think time needs to be committed to these young people to offer them support and to have any chance of effecting change, but at the moment, we're just so stretched; it's so difficult.' (Site B, senior leader)

However, small changes were starting to be made to practice processes with young people who were being interviewed by police and social workers following concerns about exploitation or peer abuse. Timescales for interviews had been extended, young people had been offered choice in respect of when/where they met professionals for interview and redesign work had been considered for buildings where interviews took place, so that they felt welcoming, safe and comfortable for young people. To implement these changes, professionals in that part of the service required adaptation to their workloads, and this, in turn, had cost implications. All of this work positioned this part of the service outside of standard practices and systems, and demonstrated that for the service to be trauma informed, key elements of how it functioned required significant modification.

We had agreed with the sites at the start of the fieldwork that we would provide a summary report at the end of each time period of data collection, offering our reflections on how the implementation could be further facilitated. A fundamental question that we raised in our report at the end of the first time period was how each site might now move beyond a simple training-oriented change process, with the aim of improving individual practice, towards creating a system that could embed the new practice principles consistently over time and ensure that practitioners were supported in practising in trauma-informed ways.

One feedback point we offered for sites' consideration was the potential value of fleshing out the bones of their theory of change to enable them to be clearer about what was needed to ensure practitioners could progress from thinking differently to doing differently. A second suggestion was that they might offer clinical support or supervision and other group spaces where staff could reflect on the emotional impact of the work with young people. The benefits of this at a practical level would mean that the challenges of working in a trauma-informed way could be better identified and strategies shared. Just as importantly but less tangibly, the experience of trauma-informed supervision-in-action in reflexive individual or group spaces would facilitate 'deep learning' of the new approach (Clare, 2007) and enable workers to better process secondary trauma and develop vicarious resilience (Méndez-Fernández et al, 2022).

Moving towards innovation

In the second time period of data collection in Site B, we were able to observe further elements of system- and service-wide transformation rooted in the principles of Trauma-informed Practice. Specific structures within the service were reformed, such as the multi-agency child exploitation panels, where risk assessment and planning for young people took place. Unlike with the more modest examples of improvement noted earlier, Trauma-informed Practice had now become evident across the whole panel process, rather than being something only displayed at discrete moments by individual practitioners. For example, rather than an individual practitioner taking the initiative to foreground a young person's likes and dislikes, the panel chair and the panel structure required that this be the approach on every occasion. The questions asked of panel members directed their attention to contextual factors, recognised young people's choice, desire for trust and need for safety, and identified opportunities for collaboration. By framing meetings in this way, the ethos of children's social care also informed the approach of the wider partnership. As multi-agency partners were engaged over time in a panel structure that was trauma informed, this, in turn, gradually shifted the culture. We observed changes in language, attitudes to young people and panel recommendations that were more aligned with trauma-informed principles, including:

- efforts to reflect on the humanity of the young person – their likes, dislikes, hope and ambitions – beyond the risks they faced/posed (empowerment);
- discussions about safety, and evidence of pockets of safety and survival in the young person's life, despite wider risks (safety);
- advocacy to pursue services or interventions that the young person had wanted, and to challenge those that the young person had described as unhelpful, including within other agencies, such as schools or the police (choice/trust); and
- attempts to secure service responses that went beyond what was normally provided, for example, extending the length of time a worker was allocated to a young person, as this was the only individual that they trusted (choice/trust).

The examples of practice improvement cited earlier in the chapter could be described as innovative in character: changing the tone of meetings for short periods of time or unsettling the usual pattern of professional decision making in individual cases was disruptive at a micro-level. While they did not constitute sustained system innovation, they opened up a potential pathway to further transformation.

As Site B moved towards pursuing system reform, they also recognised the additional costs of this exercise. Senior leaders who had been previously reassured that the new approach would be low cost were later informed that the reduced caseloads and reflective spaces necessary to Trauma-informed Practice would, in fact, require additional ongoing finance. Propitiously, the collaboration with our project had generated data indicating that the incremental system changes already made were starting to shift cultures and practices; those leading the innovation were able to use these data to build a case to justify the necessity of increasing resources. The senior leadership buy-in that resulted was pivotal for reform in Site B, as it facilitated further steps towards innovative implementation, including the introduction of additional steps to reduce practitioner anxiety around high-risk work and to ensure professionals felt safe to develop alternative responses or challenge each other. For example, pre-panel consultations were introduced for social workers to talk through the situations their young people faced prior to discussions at panels. Such work created the space for panels to be focused on safety and welfare, rather than solely concerned with risk, and, in this process, be more reflective of Trauma-informed Practice.

By the third time period, we saw that these movements in cultures and practices had started to gain momentum. Yet, Site B remained fully cognisant that they were on a longer-term innovation journey, with much left to achieve and embed across their systems:

'So, well, obviously, I think it's a long-term plan. … We've built in awareness of what it means to be trauma informed into the practice, into offers of training, our induction, our post-qualifying year, you know, so we're kind of weaving it in as an underpinning approach to everything that we're trying to do. So, so, we're on that journey … but I couldn't say with any confidence the whole workforce is really trauma informed in their practice, and we're certainly not at a point where we can be saying what a difference it's making … so that's still a work in progress.' (Site B, senior leader)

Comparatively, in Site A, the 'continuous improvement' approach meant the introduction of Trauma-informed Practice was viewed as a mid-range goal, something with a clear end point and something that could still be achieved via a small number of discrete tasks (such as training), which individuals could adopt through improvements to their own practice, while wider systems remained relatively unchanged. There are challenges with this interpretation. First, it places significant responsibility on individual practitioners to implement an approach that requires multi-agency and (to an extent) wider system take-up. Second, it does not account for the additional time, effort and capacity that it may take even for this individually oriented improvement to be embedded given the degree of staff churn, high workloads and rigid systems that are common to statutory services and that individual practitioners or teams have little control over. Within a continuous improvement model, change processes are potentially constrained indefinitely by an outer shell of a system that may itself be perpetuating the practice problem that requires improvement. Where Trauma-informed Practice is viewed as an innovation that, by definition, invites a re-envisioning of paradigms and systems, it has the potential to change the conditions in which social care is practised, not solely the practice of social workers.

Conclusion

In this chapter, we have discussed how efforts to implement Trauma-informed Practice in two sites reflected both facets of incremental service improvement and whole-system innovation. Our study suggests that both innovation and improvement – whether they be offered as a concept, model or set of processes – are potentially helpful strategies for changing practices and systems. They can open up conversations about what is possible to achieve that will be better than what went before, galvanise people towards a common cause and potentially help services to structure a process to achieve their aims. What became clear in this research, however, is that there are limitations regarding what incremental improvement can achieve within the constraints of an existing system shell. It was only as system redesign work began in Site B that we could see not only the innovative potential of Trauma-informed Practice but also why it was necessary to go beyond improvement processes: individual practice can only ever be truly trauma informed if it is delivered through a whole service structured around that ethos. This point has more general relevance for the introduction of Trauma-informed Practice for other areas of public services and – as can be seen through other chapters in this book – more broadly in the field of extra-familial risks and harms, where existing policy frameworks and macro-practice systems may not only constrain youth-centred and relational practices but also intensify the difficulties that practitioners experience in providing the practice conditions that young people require and demand.

Key chapter insights for policy and practice

- Services need to determine whether the enhanced efficiency and effectiveness of services can be achieved through incremental practice improvement measures or whether a more fundamental rethinking of paradigms and systems (innovation) is required.
- Distinctions between 'continuous improvement' and actual innovation are not always clear-cut, and the former may sometimes 'scaffold' the introduction of the latter.

- The framework of principles associated with Trauma-informed Practice needs to be interpreted and tailored to each specific context and set of delivery aims.
- The promise that Trauma-informed Practice offers cannot be realised without fundamental changes to organisational systems (requiring innovation), and this may demand more in terms of resources.

FIVE

What 'works' in innovation?

Introduction

During an observation of a meeting held within one of our case-study sites, a senior member of the organisation remarked, "We know that Contextual Safeguarding works, but we need to be able to evidence it". We had been invited to observe a discussion on developing an outcomes framework for the new system they were testing, which was rooted in Contextual Safeguarding principles. During the meeting, we were particularly struck by this comment that Contextual Safeguarding 'worked'. Despite some of us having been involved for many years (in other capacities) with the frameworks of Trauma-informed Practice, Transitional Safeguarding and Contextual Safeguarding, we have never, ourselves, asserted with such confidence that they 'work'. This was not an isolated example. Across various other of our case-study sites, practitioners and leaders echoed a similar idea: the new intervention or system being introduced either 'works' or 'should work'.

What leads professionals to make these claims? Perhaps the 'common sense' promise that a new framework offers or its ethical compatibility with the social care sector encourage a type of confirmation bias (Oeij et al, 2019). Otherwise, maybe the professional quoted earlier had seen evidence that we had not. A more likely explanation is that the innovation contexts themselves create pressure on those involved to 'perform' successful innovation processes and achieve aspired outcomes. Definitions of social innovation share a similar vision of achieving better outcomes, improving lives and benefiting society, and it is recognised that significant investments of time, resources, funding and personal and emotional energy will be required to put this into play (Mulgan et al, 2007; Murray et al, 2010; Young Foundation, 2012). It is, then, unsurprising that not only innovators but also funders, commissioners and national and local government feel pressure to demonstrate that new practice systems or methods 'work' in order to justify the investment of public resources. Indeed, in the UK, a centre dedicated to 'What Works for Children & Families' (Foundations, 2023) is the latest manifestation of a long-standing requirement for social work to prove its legitimacy as a profession, underpinned by a decontextualised view of interventions, the best of which carry a so-called 'gold standard' evidence base (Mosley et al, 2019). Is it any wonder that professionals and researchers – even if unconsciously – feel the pressure to emphasise success and minimise the failures of their innovation activity?

In this chapter, we focus both on what work is required to 'perform' innovation and what factors come into play in determining whether it 'works'. In this chapter, we use 'work' (in inverted commas) to denote 'producing successful outcomes'. Conversely, drawing on Smith's definition of the term from institutional ethnography (Smith and Griffith, 2022), we use work (without inverted commas) more expansively and fluidly to explore the practices of professionals and researchers engaged in the process of innovation, and the connections these practices have to wider discourses. Returning to the professional quoted earlier in this chapter, our aim is not to prove them wrong but to highlight how emotional and discursive practices – for example, believing in and promoting innovation – are important players in the innovation process.

The context itself shapes such performances through a range of external influences and drivers. Again drawing on the work of institutional ethnography, we refer to these as examples of the 'ruling relations [that] impose their objectified modes upon us' (Smith and Griffith, 2022: 7). To understand these ruling relations, we look across the innovation activity in our case-study sites to explore the work that went into considering whether or how the three innovation frameworks (Contextual Safeguarding, Transitional Safeguarding and Trauma-informed Practice) had 'worked'.

This chapter explores these contexts and the conditions that propel researchers and professionals towards performing success. In doing so, we ask if the aspired outcomes of these three innovation frameworks are even possible to achieve and, if not, what happens when there is a disconnect between a belief that a new system or intervention should work and evidence that it does not, or even cannot, work. We focus particularly on the boundary between organisational challenges that may enable or inhibit innovation success and the emotional and psychological experiences of practitioners tasked with implementing innovation. Our aim by so doing is to unearth the work of professionals that, while vital, is often hidden. We want to speak back to the mounting pressure practitioners and researchers are under to demonstrate quantifiable success and explore the limitations that this places on them, as well as on the ability of the sector, to truly learn about, and engage with, the context of innovation.

We conclude our introduction with a short illustrative story. In the final year of the Innovate Project, as a requirement of our annual reporting, a senior member of the research team asked us all to consider and record for the funder any evidence that our research had led to ascertainable benefits to the public (for example, the policy or practice field, young people, or families). We tried to think of any of the direct or tenuous ways our activities, publications and resources might have helped people, and obediently recorded these in a spreadsheet. While many familiar with public services in contexts of neoliberalism will not be surprised by a request to measure and quantify the value of work, we share this to show that we, as researchers, like the practitioner earlier in this chapter, are equally caught up in this performance, this dance to show that our activity 'works'.

What are we doing when we innovate?

The primary task

When faced with the prospect of engaging in social innovation, it is likely that, at some point, all participants will be faced with the question, 'What are we doing?'. While this question might be a practical one, it is more likely to be philosophical in nature: 'What exactly is the task at hand?'. To understand the work required in innovation practice, we draw on the concept of the 'primary task' in seeking to understand how organisations order, prioritise and understand collective tasks (Lawrence, 1977; Miller and Rice; 2013; Owens, 2015). There are three ways of considering a group's task: the 'normative', 'existential' and 'phenomenal'. The normative task is the stated task of the group. In the Innovate Project, for example, our normative task was to research practice and system innovation associated with three frameworks – Contextual Safeguarding, Trauma-informed Practice and Transitional Safeguarding – to better understand the processes of innovation and improve safeguarding responses to young people experiencing extra-familial risks and harms. While the normative task is conscious, the existential and phenomenal are unconscious. Lawrence (1977) outlines how the existential task is what the group think they are doing, while the phenomenal is what they actually do (Owens, 2015).

Using these concepts, we explored data across the project, focusing specifically on interviews held with key professionals leading innovation in the case-study sites. While we focus primarily on interviews with those authorising, guiding or coordinating innovation activities, we contextualised these with examples from the wider data-collection activities. Looking across this data set, we focused down on the following aspects: the existential and phenomenal tasks; the work that was undertaken to perform these tasks; and the ruling relations that shaped the conceptions and activities.

A note should be provided before we begin. There is something inherently problematic about the concept of the primary task and specifically the phenomenal task. As we reflected in Chapter One, the idea that 'we', as academic outsiders, should be making judgements about what practitioners (who work extremely hard under challenging circumstances) *really* do feels uncomfortable, at best, and unfair, at worst. Therefore, we have sought to surface throughout this chapter (and the book as a whole) how we ourselves were influenced by the ruling relations; we bring wider systemic and structural powers into focus, and explore these concepts in relation to principles of ethical and psychosocially informed approaches. It is in the spirit of understanding and solidarity that we hope to shine a light on the hidden aspects of everyday work, particularly when it comes to the complex work involved in the performance of innovation.

What we think we are doing: the existential task

What do professionals think they are doing when they embark on the introduction of new practice methods and systems to respond to extra-familial risks and harms? In this section, we seek to reach beyond descriptions of activity and outcomes (the normative tasks) towards something grounded in the 'doings' of professionals (we include researchers in this group) to get closer to considering what is happening at an existential and less conscious level. Looking back on observations and interviews with those responsible for leading and progressing innovation, we have often wondered: 'What is it that they think they are doing?'. Of course, this is only half the story because their innovation work and our research ethnography did not happen in a vacuum. To properly excavate the existential tasks, we needed to look at not only what happened in the case-study sites but also how we (the researchers) have been integral to the doing and performing of this innovation activity.

The existential task that dominated our analysis was that professionals thought it was their 'responsibility' to progress the innovation journey and even, as one professional noted, to "believe" in the potential benefits of the chosen framework and how it had been translated into systems or interventions: "I very much see myself in a bit of a facilitator [role] ... no, I don't know if that's the right word ... flying the flag!" (local leader). For many, their sense of duty to keep the innovation journey alive was experienced within a wider organisational environment where they, as individuals, felt isolated in this task and very much at the vanguard of the boundaries of their system, pushing at its ability to change. One person described themselves as a "maverick", and several others saw themselves as always involved in trying to bring about change. However, occupying this position came at a cost. Professionals spoke about their roles and tasks in very personal terms; they displayed a strong sense of moral duty to the work of enabling the new practice methods and systems to flourish and sustain in their local area.

As research staff, our task was not as directly implicated in the holding and carrying work of innovation, but it did include some of these preoccupations. For example, at points through our study, 'jokes' arose within the research team about which of the three research strands (Contextual Safeguarding, Transitional Safeguarding and Trauma-informed Practice) was 'performing' the best – for example, who had collected the most data. This was never an official process but rather a cultural and affective manifestation of our preoccupations; we too were caught up in an unconscious existential task that was to do with how well we were performing. Like the professionals in the case-study sites, our response to this task was to double down on work – hard work – to take away the feeling that if there was anything amiss, it was not because of our lack of effort. In other words, the investment in the implementation of the innovation frameworks as something precious and in the task of dutifully guarding them was just as alive in the research team as it was with professionals in practice.

As well as bringing our own preoccupations about our performance into the system, we saw in the fieldwork how anxiety about innovation performance in sites was transferred unconsciously (Klein, 1952) between practitioners and the research staff. For example, at times, the researchers' task seemed to focus on validating and acknowledging the work of professionals. Perhaps we sensed the absence of other forms of acknowledgement within the professionals' system, or we wanted to ameliorate guilt at asking hard-working professionals to account for their innovation activity. It could even have been to comfort and reassure both researcher and professional that they/we were doing a good job in the face of a lack of obvious progress. Probably, it was a mix of all three. However, if we take it that their/our existential task was to hold alive the innovation endeavour within contexts variously hostile to this process, it makes sense that, as researchers, we might feel compelled to appreciate the work of professionals caught in this tension.

The extent to which the case-study sites were successful in keeping alive their innovations and getting them to grow differed. In one site, where a local leader felt that the innovation goals had not been accomplished, the landscape of her interview was full of the existential language of death and destruction, and she described herself as "sound[ing] a bit martyring". Across the research strands, there were examples where those leading or coordinating innovation activity felt that they were holding personal responsibility. Indeed, the implication that a particular individual might represent and be accountable for the success of the innovation activity was embedded within the research methods. An example of this is apparent in our interview topic guide, which included asking local leaders to assess their site's progress in operationalising their innovation framework on a scale of 1 to 5, where 5 was 'fully implemented'. Underlying this question was a shared assumption that sites should be striving towards a 5, with leaders being asked to rate their progress again at subsequent data-collection points.

Despite our best intentions towards reflexivity, as researchers, we were co-opted into the existential task of keeping alive the introduction of the new practice method or system. While in Chapter Three, we explored how understanding innovation as a recursive activity could relieve us from false expectations of 'completion', the question of whether we could contemplate the prospect of failure without recovery remained. In the interview with the professional who used the expression of "martyring", she and the researcher seemed to share a hope that, despite perceptions and concerns about failure at that point, the introduction of the new practice system or method might yet come to fruition at some future point. It was as if the notion that it might not was too hard to think about – too existential and nihilistic. Looked at this way, perhaps, at an unconscious level, what we (both researchers and practitioners) think we are doing is proving that all is not lost – that social care can be reformed and change is possible.

This is a heavy existential task to bear. Throughout the interviews, professionals spent considerable time justifying, defending and querying whether they had gone about their work in the right way, whether they had influenced the right people and whether they had built the right relationships. They questioned both themselves and the enormity of the scope of the innovation. For example, in the following extract, a researcher and local leader stumble on the issue of the parameters of the innovation:

Leader:	'What do you mean by "organisation" again? So, we're talking about–?'
Researcher:	'[Name of council.]'
Leader:	'The council as a whole?'

Researcher: 'Yeah, yeah, or children's services specifically.'
Leader: 'Oh, children's services, right, OK.'

The next two examples represent local leaders' heavy personal feelings associated with the innovation task:

> 'I genuinely hope it [the innovation framework] succeeds at some point. I'm going to be incredibly jealous of the person who does actually get it to succeed!' (Local manager)

> 'The things I'm struggling with is, like, I've got, like, my last meeting with [colleague] at 4 o'clock just to. … [I'm] feeling, like, a bit of guilt around leaving them holding things in quite a precarious position.' (Team manager)

What comes through strongly when these extracts are set alongside each other is the personal responsibility of individuals grappling with their task. Why was the cost of the existential task held so personally, despite them being, by their very nature, about systemic change? Turning to institutional ethnography, this can be illuminated by thinking about the ruling relations, which may be uncovered by following lines of enquiry from the data about the institutional structures that govern and dictate the 'doings' of people. Foregrounding the systemic and structural features of social care highlights their significance in helping the move from the existential tasks (what we think we are doing) towards the phenomenal tasks (what we are really doing) because of the way they contextualise the innovation process. By way of example, the following quotes touch on the impact of policy and organisational challenges, including inspection, restructuring and underfunding, on this process:

> 'And I think a number of things have also happened for us that have, maybe, have put us on a back foot and delayed us a little bit; so, Ofsted being one of them. So, I think,

you know, when Ofsted come, everything stops, doesn't it, really … you know the two weeks before, and then the few days that they're here, and then the week after because you're trying to recover.' (Local leader)

'So, my role was to be a project lead for introducing and embedding the [innovation]. And then that role was probably in place for a year and … then the funding stopped for that role, and I moved into another role, and I was promoted in those various roles. But the legacy of that work or the responsibility of that work I retained.' (Team manager)

'The staff are in trauma because they're having to move to new buildings and a new way of working, and we haven't got all the buildings yet geared up to that.' (Service manager)

If we situate the existential tasks set out earlier alongside these ruling relations, we see that professionals and researchers are often engaged in a task of keeping innovations alive within a wider environment that is hostile to their taking root and growing. When they experience problems with this process, the nature of the existential task drives them to negative comparison and self-doubt. The collective wish to have done a good job, to have made a positive contribution, can overwhelm our ability to consider that, despite our best efforts and intentions, the conditions may not allow the good thing we want to bring about to happen. It may sometimes lead us to an even more problematic task of making it look like a new intervention or system is working, even where we lack evidence for such claims. This disconnect between what we think (and wish) we are doing and what we actually are doing is where we will dive in next.

What we are really doing: phenomenal tasks

The task of keeping the innovation activity alive, or 'flying the flag', was undoubtedly made easier by the fact that the majority of those tasked with doing so believed in the principles and ethics that underpinned the three frameworks for innovation that were being operationalised in the case-study sites. It was this belief that guided a desire for them to want to see them 'work'. Professionals viewed the frameworks for innovation as variously common sense, a platform for bigger change and/or exciting: Contextual Safeguarding was referred to as "bloody obvious"; Transitional Safeguarding was believed to offer the means to "make significant changes across the whole organisation"; and one professional commented, "Nobody has ever said being trauma informed isn't a good idea". However, belief in the underlying values and a proven ability of these three innovation frameworks to improve experiences and outcomes for young people experiencing risk or harm are not the same thing.

Professionals spoke extensively about the challenges they experienced in embedding the chosen innovation framework and the new practice methods and systems it had spawned, including funding, leadership, inspections and bureaucracy. However, despite recognising the disconnect between their belief that the innovations should 'work' and a lack of evidence of that, this did not lead them to doubt the innovation frameworks themselves or whether they were possible to implement. If your primary task is based on the belief that the innovations will 'work', what do you do when the evidence you are presented with is that they have not 'worked' or may not work in your organisation? The phenomenal task, or the answer to the question 'What are we really doing?', is perhaps then avoiding talking about whether innovation frameworks themselves 'work' – in other words, ignoring the disconnect between what is hoped for and what is possible. In this final section, we consider the phenomenal task by asking, 'What if the innovations cannot 'work' and what is the cost of not asking this question?'.

The cost it seems, as we saw in the previous section, is that professionals try to fill the gap themselves, often at a personal cost. Innovation leaders discussed their sense of guilt and dismay at the limited progress of their innovation project, and even recognised feelings of jealousy that someone else might be able to bring something to fruition that they had not. It was not, of course, a total picture of failure. Many felt that they were successfully embedding the innovations. In these sites, success was viewed as the result of the strengths of individual endeavours. Across the study, innovation leaders frequently asked us if other local authorities were implementing the innovation frameworks successfully and, if so, how were they achieving this. They looked for validation from our research team that others were also struggling to find practical solutions. However, they also had a seemingly genuine desire to hear of positive examples that they themselves could draw on, and we, also deeply invested, tried to meet their needs. We spoke of the struggles of other sites and tried to face up to difficult questions about the practical things people were doing in practice.

Instead of asking what factors and processes enable or inhibit innovations in sites, we turn now to asking, 'What if these innovation frameworks do not/cannot work?'. What does this allow us to learn about social work today when seemingly common-sense approaches are so hard to implement? If we accept that Contextual Safeguarding, Trauma-informed Practice and Transitional Safeguarding should, in theory, work but are rarely presented with robust evidence of them being fully implemented or successful in addressing extra-familial risks and harms, we need to ask if it is ethical to bring them into social care departments, where the conditions may not be conducive to their successful development. This is not only because of the personal cost to those practitioners developing the work but because those likely to experience new systems or approaches that may not be beneficial or effective – young people and families – are some of the most marginalised in our societies.

We consider five provocations that could help our understanding of why these innovations might not, or cannot, 'work' (it should be noted how, even as we write this, we are fearful to write the more assertive 'do not work'). First, the three innovation frameworks are premised on ethical and socially just approaches to working with young people. They require – as an absolute baseline – practitioners and services to care about young people and feel they have a right to safety. This is so much the case that with Contextual Safeguarding particularly, and with Transitional Safeguarding potentially, organisations and systems may need to increase the scope of work and the resources required to ensure that there are services for young people where there would otherwise not be. Do we, as adults, professionals, politicians, academics and the public, value young people enough to listen to them, respect them, care for them, provide them with what they need and, ultimately, put our hands in our pockets (Boddy, 2023)? Maybe the answer is 'no'; if so, that would be one reason why these new frameworks would never 'work'.

Second, these frameworks for innovation require us – even those of us who are so seemingly well intentioned – to look at how our own systems and practices inflict institutional harm. This must be done not as part of some audit process but through reflection and learning within an environment where it is safe to recognise our own limitations. We should not underestimate how challenging this is for those scrutinised by inspection frameworks and other forms of governance.

Third, what if the policy and practice infrastructure required to implement these frameworks is not sufficiently developed for authorities to utilise them? While there are differing principles and resources available for the three frameworks, they are not manualised, and arguably should not be. Is it just too early for the type of change proposed by these three frameworks?

Fourth, perhaps it is not possible to transfer principles from a strengths-based framework into social care systems that are often experienced by families and young people as surveilling, punishing and uncaring rather than supportive (Roberts et al, 2021), and where social workers and their decisions are scrutinised and assessed too. Finally, what if practitioners cannot see that the way they have interpreted and implemented the innovation frameworks are misaligned with their original intentions? Many practitioners and professionals we spoke with illustrated their accounts with positive examples of the way their local innovations were 'working'. However, sometimes, the evidence we were presented with seemed to conflict with this, as we set out in one of our other project outputs (Firmin et al, forthcoming).

If there is any 'truth' to these provocations, then where do we go from here? First, we need to reflect, both individually and collectively, on our personal views and what we are/are not doing. In considering what it means for professionals to really care for, like or even love young people in the context of social care (for example, The Promise, Scotland, 2020), we all must ask ourselves, 'Do *we* care sufficiently about young people *and* actively demonstrate that care?', Second, we need to consider how we can more consistently apply a strengths–based approach and what possibilities this may open up. Finally, we (policy makers, professionals and researchers) need to create a practice environment that encourages and supports practitioners to stay true to values of social justice. We conclude with considering the implications of these points, asking, 'What is it we cannot say?'.

Boundary transgressions and vested interests

Continuing a commitment to exploring parallel processes between the innovation sites and research team, it is not just practitioners who avoid questioning if the innovation frameworks or their local implementations 'work'. After completing the data analysis for this chapter and identifying the themes, one of the authors stated: "The problem is, we need to be careful not to imply that the innovations *don't* work." Even as we write this, we sit uncomfortably with the idea that our critique might be used by some to dismiss these three innovation frameworks. As researchers, we are emotionally and socially committed to seeing that the public money invested in the practice sites and in our funded research project is used to good effect. Perhaps, in part, this is because we want to justify our existence. However, perhaps more importantly, we have all been drawn to this field because of our shared ethic of care and commitment to social justice: we want to help improve conditions for disadvantaged and vulnerable young people and their families. To this end, as researchers, we have at times stepped beyond the ethnographic outsider role envisaged by Smith (2005), where it would have been expected that we should observe without influence; instead, we have reflected back to our sites, at various points, what we were seeing and learning in order to support them on their journeys. If, when and how to do so was not a straightforward decision for us; however, ultimately, it would have 'felt' unethical not to do so – although it would have been perfectly within the bounds of our original research design. To coin a phrase, the personal and political, then, is methodological.

Some members of our research team have also been led to reflect on the extent to which we had a more personal investment in uncovering clear evidence that one or other of the innovation frameworks 'works', or at least offers strong promise. Where we had held a pivotal role in developing the underpinning innovation framework, we might also be fearful that, in acknowledging a current lack of evidence, or in even asking, 'What if this framework might not "work"?', we might lose funding, lose our jobs or lose credibility. As for innovators, so too for researchers: where a gap between theory, practice and evidence might be filled with personal cost, system conditions that allow for honesty, transparency and critical reflection become ever more essential.

Conclusion

What we have explored in this chapter is how innovation in social care involves professionals and researchers in a complex set of often unconscious and anxiety-laden tasks. At the existential level, we are preoccupied with responding to the neoliberal ruling relations that cause us to perform innovation success. Rather than acknowledging these relations, we enact defences against the unbearable thought that the context might be too hostile for innovation to take root and make a difference by working hard and often carrying emotional loads that are very difficult to bear. The aim of this chapter has been to support those involved in innovation to reach a more 'depressive' (Klein, 1952) or realistic position, which might include asking if these innovations are possible. This is about going beyond holding individuals to account for the failure or success of innovation. It requires a deeper examination of the way that defences are enacted at an organisational and systemic level.

Key chapter insights for policy and practice

- Practitioners and researchers are caught within neoliberal 'ruling relations' that lead them to seek to perform innovation success.
- Innovation successes and failures are often attributed to individuals rather than focusing on the organisational context that can facilitate or inhibit them.
- Practitioners and researchers need to be supported to safely consider if and why innovations are/are not successful. They should ask:
  - What needs to change about the frameworks or local innovations to support them to 'work'?
  - What needs to change about the ruling relations that govern the contexts in which they are developed to make progress possible?'

SIX

Innovation and organisational defences

Introduction

Innovation in social care involves changing paradigms, systems and practices, often quite radically. When it comes to the field of extra-familial risks and harms, some of these changes have been rapid and recent. Particularly in the case of Contextual Safeguarding, new ways of working, with new partners, have emerged with increasing volition in response to harms that not long ago were thought to be irrelevant for children's social care. With such rapid growth and transformation, how can innovation practice ensure that it keeps young people central to vision, design and review? Might an innovation designed to safeguard young people at risk beyond the home, no matter how well meaning, at times override young people's rights and agency, their ways of seeing the world, their perspectives, and their wider welfare needs? And why might this happen?

So far in this book, we have argued that innovation, particularly in the area of extra-familial risks and harms, should be approached with consideration and care: in Chapter Two, we discussed the importance of having the right conditions for innovation; in Chapter Three, we explored the delicacy associated with early-stage innovation; and in Chapter Five, we looked at the high personal cost to practitioners of maintaining a narrative of innovation success when innovation conditions are not right. In this chapter, we pick up this cautionary theme to explore how innovation can lead to defensive practices that alienate young people and could cause them further harm. Taking up Brown's (2015) encouragement to be honest about innovation 'failure', we look again at the gap (identified in Chapter Five) between a wish to innovate, on the one hand, and the reality of what is possible, on the other. Rather than thinking about the impact on practitioners, we now analyse what happens to organisational systems when they lack the space to reflect on the mismatch between innovation vision and its reality.

A framework for thinking about organisational defences

Turning to the psychosocial concept of 'social systems as a defence against anxiety' (Menzies-Lyth, 1988 [1959]), this chapter will explore the defences that emerge when innovation is implemented without the policies, resources and culture to enable it to flourish. Using examples from our data, we go on to show how complex anxieties 'beneath the surface' within the collective organisational unconscious can lead to practices that can have significant and tangible consequences for the services that young people receive.

As with Chapter Five, this territory comes with a degree of caution. We are not psychoanalysts, and nor is it our role to pathologise practitioners or their practice. We start from the position that, as with individual psychological defences, social and organisational defences exist because they are necessary. Particularly when it comes to work that involves serious harm and death to young people, it makes sense that we, as humans, need a way to defend ourselves against these crushing and painful realities, as well as the limited degree to which we can prevent them. Individually, defences can lead us to avoiding feeling things it might be better we felt. This avoidance can stop us from taking advantage of opportunities and limit us in many ways. Shifting to thinking about organisations and groups, similar dysfunctional defence structures can be at play. As with individual defences, their purpose is often to protect organisations, but they risk preventing the organisation's members from connecting with emotions in ways that limit the organisation's capacity to fulfil its mission. This links back to the idea of the primary task explored in Chapter Five. We could say that the primary task of the case-study organisations involved with the Innovate Project is to promote young people's well-being by protecting them from risk and harm beyond their family settings. How does this primary task mobilise organisational defences, and, in institutional ethnography terms, how do such defences manifest and concretise in organisational policies, procedures and forms of governance? What work (Smith and Griffith, 2022) do these defences do in creating or maintaining certain forms of discourse about young people or particular cultures of practice? These questions are the focus of this chapter.

To start, it is useful to foreground the role of psychological containment and its role in group defences. Again, we draw on theoretical frameworks developed from the study of individual psychological processes and later applied to group processes. The foundation of this work comes from Bion (1962), who studied the way that a mother might take in, and hold, the strong feelings projected into them by their baby – a process termed 'reverie'. Containment is about holding feelings, but, crucially, feelings are not just given over to be evacuated by the containing person. Rather, Bion describes how an infant's emotions are made more tolerable through reverie: feelings are 'passed back' to the baby in a less scary form, helping them to tolerate what previously was intolerable. What makes this possible is the adult capacity of the mother, who can 'internalise a container of feelings but also a mind that can hold thoughts' (Salzberger-Wittenberg, 1983: 60). As with defences, containment is a concept that has been taken up in common discourse within the social care sector, but here we want to define it more precisely than simply listening empathetically. Applied beyond infant/child processes, containment within group processes is about how complex, unconsciously held, unsettling, 'unwanted or threatening ideas' (Frosh, 2012: 162) – which may be mobilised by intolerable anxieties provoked by the primary task – can be 'taken in' by the thinking mind of the organisation. Applied specifically to social care, Ruch (2007: 662) addresses this question to argue for the need for 'safe' spaces for social workers and managers to 'make sense of the uncertainty and anxiety they encounter on an everyday basis'. As we explore in the following, in the absence of such safe spaces, intolerable anxieties can be defended against through off-task, and even harmful, activities.

The framework we developed to analyse practice within the case-study sites was informed by Menzies-Lyth's (1988 [1959]) work and also draws on related ideas from Cooper and Lees (2015). Menzies-Lyth's work arose out of an observational study of a hospital in response to the 'poor quality care of patients, poor inter-relations between senior nurses and trainee nurses, and high levels of sickness and attrition rates among nurses' (Finch and Schaub, 2015: 312). She found that in the absence of emotional containment, close physical contact with suffering and dying patients had led to defensive organisational practices. Examples included obsessional activity undertaken ritualistically, such as paying considerable attention to how sheets were folded in a cupboard or the use of language that served to distance nurses from the personhood of patients, for example, using the term 'the cancer in bed five' rather than the person's name. Cooper and Lees (2015) explain that these can be thought about as 'depressive anxieties' that draw on Kleinian object-relations theory (Klein, 1973 [1955]), as what is being defended against is, in essence, 'fears about harm done to the "other", and the consequent fear of guilt about such harm' (Cooper and Lees, 2015: 244). We looked across the data from all six case studies for examples of depressive anxieties under the following categories:

- fragmentation of relationships (emotional distance between worker and young person) or depersonalised services;
- ritualised task performance (obsessional ritualistic tasks); and
- inappropriate allocation of responsibility (offloading of decisions upwards or criticising downwards) (Ruch, 2007).

Cooper and Lees (2015: 248) argue that public scrutiny, inspection, political sensitivity and the marketisation of public services have led to a new set of anxieties that, rather than being linked to close contact with vulnerable children and their experiences of suffering, are generated by external pressures that 'bear down' on organisations with 'a life of their own'. Mindful of the extra-organisational features at play in the policy context of extra-familial harm and the scrutiny linked to innovation research, we added the following 'persecutory' anxieties to our analysis framework:

- rationing anxieties (worries about resources, cuts and so on);
- performance anxieties (motivated by data, audits and service inspections); and
- partnership anxieties (networks of multi-agencies over which no one has central control).

We chose two examples of data from each case-study site: an observation of practice and a discussion with practitioners (interview, focus group or collaborative meeting). Alongside considering the features of depressive and persecutory anxieties, we also asked a key institutional ethnography question: in whose interests is this work happening (Rankin, 2017)? To exemplify our findings, we present two composite vignettes drawn from the data analysed. Everything represented in the vignettes was witnessed somewhere in the fieldwork. The reported conversations comprise an amalgam of: (1) paraphrased text, which has been slightly altered to preserve anonymity; and (2) transcribed verbatim speech, which is indicated by quotation marks. These constructed conversations illustrate our attempt to apprehend and appreciate how organisational systems that seek to create safety for young people affected by extra-familial risks and harms collectively manage by defending themselves against the uncertainty and anxiety generated by their primary task.

Observing organisational defences in the case-study sites

A typical extra-familial panel

Imagine the following scene. You are a social worker attending a multi-agency panel. The role of the panel is to provide oversight of the most 'high-risk cases' of young people experiencing extra-familial harm. The following discussion takes place:

Chair:	Does anyone have any updates?
Social Worker 1:	'There's quite a lot of mental health coming up' in the area at the moment.
Chair:	Ok, on that, let's move on to Craig: a 16-year-old male. They've scored 92. 'This is high at 92.'
Panel member:	How is the score made up again?
Chair:	You get '10 for suicide and self-harm'.
Social Worker 1:	'There have been incidents while he was inside.'
Youth worker:	I tried to get updates from the prison, but I haven't heard from them.
Chair:	'We need to know what's happening.'
Youth justice worker:	I had arranged to see him, but his family have moved, so I couldn't. Hopefully, I'll see him next week.
Chair:	I think we can reduce the score now he's out. 'Anything new to add from the police side?'
Police:	'He's showing as victim of another crime; is that relevant still?' 'Just whizzing through.' 'For us, he's wanted, although he's also missing.'

Chair:	We need to find out about the crime – can you confirm for next time? Shall we talk about the network?
Social worker:	'Missing is not a feature of the broader network' but 'we have young people and care leavers with a lot of safeguarding concerns'. There's exploitation happening with the girls.
Chair (to social worker):	Have you updated the safety plan and risk rating? 'What we as an organisation need to know is that we've got a line of sight to our most at risk.' Do we have any more intel on the network?
Police:	'Last week they were found with a peer in possession of substances. They were NFA'd [no further action]. I overruled because I don't agree it's not in the public interest to pursue it. I'm pleased to say this will now get a response.'
Chair:	'Thank you. I'm glad to hear they will get a youth offending response which will be welfare led.'

Distance and fragmentation

If you have never been involved in a panel like this, you might be disturbed or confused by what is going on. At the start of the vignette, the professionals are talking about the mental health of young people in their local area. They then focus on a young person – Craig – who, during his time in prison, attempted to kill or harm himself. They discuss how Craig has recently been the victim of a crime and has been hurt, but they do not know how. Neither do they know where Craig is. Although Craig's friends are not missing, professionals are worried that harm and abuse might happen to them. Craig's safety is very uncertain, and the way to help him is unclear. Even writing about this now and imagining Craig as a real young man makes us feel worried for him. Yet, the language used in the vignette – reflecting what we saw in observations – does not convey these emotions but, rather, seems to work as a defence.

Depersonalised language and processes that created distance rather than connection between young people and workers were something we saw across the ethnography. In the vignette, converting suicide into a quantifiable number, using phrases or words like "mental health coming up", "missing", "wanted", "networks" and "safeguarding", and referring to Craig as a "male", all function to separate the professionals from what is really happening and its human nature. They convey no emotion. The term "missing" is shorthand for a range of statutory processes and time frames, but it also means that there is a young person out there at risk of harm and the people in the room do not know where he is. Professionals say "there's exploitation happening" to avoid saying young people are being raped for money. Following Menzies-Lyth's thinking, we ask: what underlies the systemic use of euphemistic, matter-of-fact, technical responses to violence and abuse towards young people? We sense that this is a 'depressive' anxiety, resulting from having responsibility for the safety of young people in such precarious positions when the way to help is so unclear. To deal with this, a discourse around extra-familial risks and harms has developed that masks its horror and staves off overwhelming despair. Bolstering this defence involves the practice of prioritising information gathering about young people over building relationships with them. Meetings are then dominated by following up fragments of information about young people that professionals seem to only have snippets of knowledge about, leading to a sense of things happening in the abstract. That these activities seem so far from creating safer lives for young people emphasises how they exist to make an otherwise intolerable burden of guilt and worry somewhat more tolerable for those tasked with this work.

Risk-related rituals

Alongside depersonalising and distancing practices, we also saw defences around routinised process: the updating of risk registers and safety plans, and the tyranny of producing visual maps on screens that detail 'associations' between young people (often without their knowledge), seemingly for their own sake, with little thought about whether they are necessary, accurate, useful or ethical. Routinised activities in social care are well documented (Trevithick, 2014), but what stood out was the apparent preoccupation with 'monitoring' and having 'oversight' of young people at risk beyond the home and family. The very normalisation of panels to discuss multiple young people distinguishes extra-familial risk from abuse and other harms within the family. In the last five years, such panels as multi-agency child exploitation (MACE) meetings or missing, exploited and trafficked (MET) meetings have come to dominate this landscape. Yet, these are not a feature of intra-familial safeguarding. Panels are not instigated to discuss the 15 most at-risk families on child protection plans, nor do they rely so heavily on mapping families as a primary means of intervention. What is it that is peculiar to extra-familial risks and harms that has led to a ritualised preoccupation with having a "line of sight" over young people, as referred to in this chapter's opening excerpt? Why do authorities focus on gathering "intel", the facts and "updates", and document this in such a way that it overshadows and forecloses discussions about the young people involved and their contextual needs and interests? Our sense is that while this shares many similarities to Menzies-Lyth's ritualised task performance, caused by guilt-related depressive anxieties, when it comes to extra-familial risks and harms, this is combined with persecutory preoccupations created by the wider policy context within which this work sits. This leads to a complex combination of anxieties that can preclude thinking and reflection.

Role diffusion and confusion

A feature of these multi-agency panels is the blurring of professional roles. Those whose duties focus on crime prevention often feature as primary information givers, sitting alongside those whose professional framework is in safety and welfare. In the vignette outlined earlier, there is a discussion about criminal justice agencies taking the lead in an intervention with young people, and this is described by the chair as a welfare response. Two young people at risk of harm have been found carrying drugs by police. Rather than pondering over how they came to know this (That is, were they stopped and searched and, if so, why?) or discussing who might be the best agency to respond, a senior police officer says they overturned a 'no further action' decision made by officers. No one asks what action followed from this. The chair describes it as a positive outcome.

Aside from the unexplored alternative responses, there is a striking absence of curiosity about how this might have been experienced by these young people. Are they likely to feel supported and ready to engage in a process that was instigated by police officers coming to their home or school to say that their case is reopened and they are being referred to the youth justice service? The unlikeliness of this makes it seem as if the chair's pronouncement of it being a welfare response is an act of wishful thinking, a defence against facing up to how what happened might have driven the young people further from the support they need – even if it was the only option on the table. In the absence of a more relationship- and welfare-based response, perhaps the group needed to imagine what they did was helpful, even if it might not be. This mirrors Menzies-Lyth's description of how defences can be organised around the inappropriate allocation of responsibility – the giving over of welfare work to the police. This 'depressive' anxiety is combined, however, with 'persecutory' anxieties related to networks of professionals brought together, over which no one has control (Cooper and Lees, 2015), creating a complex field of anxiety. The effect is to preclude critical and reflective thinking, enacting a powerful defence against asking whether professional activities are helping young people or, more unbearable still, might even be placing them at further risk of harm, as racially profiled stop-and-search activity has been shown to do (Jackson et al, 2021).

Defending against an untenable bind

We emphasise that defensive behaviour within the field of extra-familial risks and harms is not surprising. The combination of organisational and extra-organisational psychosocial processes is intense. Rather than judge, our intention is to seek to understand what is happening when, for example, social care professionals project wishful fantasies onto criminal justice agencies. Is it that, with extremely limited resources, the available option becomes reified as a good option? To understand this context better, let us return to the meeting:

Chair:	I'm glad to hear that these young people will have a youth offending response which will be a welfare response.
Panel member:	Was that Ryan?
Chair:	I think it's Ray-an. I always get it wrong.
Social Worker 2:	'No, but Rayan's accommodation arrangements ended last week.' The situation has escalated. Some 'males chased up to his home.' 'He had been deemed safe at his supported accommodation.' 'He was linked with an OCG [organised criminal gang]' and has 'issues with housing'.

	He was victim of an assault recently. He was beaten with a golf club. He's now 'not engaging' with 'his social worker since he left the housing project'. 'I'm really worried about him.' 'He's refusing support' but 'I'm worried' he's going to die.
Police:	'We are aware of him but it's difficult' if he isn't engaging with us.
Social Worker 2 (sounding distressed):	I've just spoken to my manager and 'the plan is to close him'.
Chair:	Because he turns 18 next week, our options are 'very limited'. We'll 'see what we can do'. 'It's difficult because he won't engage.'
Social Worker 2:	'He's scared to.' I just feel 'if we could just hold him for another one to two months'.
Police:	Is there anything else 'before we go to the tracker?'

Across the case-study sites, structures and procedures seemed to be organised in such a way that professionals could be protected from the emotional impact of the work to some degree. However, it was not the case that professionals were entirely disconnected from their feelings about the harm faced by young people. In this vignette, we also see how deeply troubled and worried many were. Social Worker 2 is in touch with depressive feelings around the danger that Rayan is in and is given some space to express care and concern. Their "if only" comment is an invitation to engage in reflective thinking: can Rayan be held for a bit longer? However, the paucity of services available overwhelms the discussion and closes down this type of thinking. There is no suitable housing for him, and he turns 18 next week. Resources are tightly rationed, and the panel must adhere to the eligibility rules around age; there is no flexibility. Although the discussion comes close to recognising that this decision might contribute to Rayan possibly dying, the system, represented by the panel, is sufficiently defended against this to 'close the case' and relinquish their responsibility for Rayan's welfare. In this way, defences against persecutory anxieties can overshadow depressive feelings to protect the organisation, person and role from their untenable bind (Cooper and Lees, 2015).

Along with the all-consuming drive to ration scarce resources, the horror of what might happen when the service stops supporting Rayan is defended against through a retreat to his lack of engagement. Rather than consider what Rayan might need and want, and to what extremes they could go to get that for him, everything is cast under the shadow of his 18th birthday. The chair and the social worker's manager adhere to the rule of the 18th birthday cut-off, and everyone else follows; they record the risk level on the 'tracker', making sure every decision is accurately recorded. In this way, the system is defended against its own neglect and dereliction of care, as well as the injury caused to workers who are required to enact such processes (Reynolds, 2011). The intra-personal, organisational and extra-organisational pressures that professionals navigate creates a toxic combination of 'depressive' and 'persecutory' anxieties and subsequent defences.

Practice within a context of uncertainty

We have painted a bleak formulation: professionals, subject to impossible conditions, unconsciously resort to defensive practices that leave young people a long way from getting what they need. Before we turn to the implications of this, we will take a deeper look at these conditions. An important factor is that these data were created by researchers (us) observing practice, primarily in online spaces. Most people being watched doing their work would likely wonder what is in the mind of the observer and perhaps worry about this. However, we suggest that the emergent and high-stakes nature of practice in the field of extra-familial risks and harms, combined with a perception in several sites that some of our research team are 'experts' in the field, created a particularly intense psychosocial affective innovation field. Here, any observational 'other' (especially a disembodied person on a screen) is likely to feed into pre-existing defences.

Central to understanding this dynamic is appreciating how safeguarding young people beyond their family settings is in a state of flux – culturally, morally and politically. Practice guidance for the three innovation frameworks (Contextual Safeguarding, Transitional Safeguarding and Trauma-informed Practice) is either in its infancy or non-existent. Regulatory and legislative frameworks for statutory practice in the field of extra-familial risks and harms are still emergent, particularly for young people in transition to adulthood. Simultaneously, there is intense media and public interest in the (anti-social) behaviour of young people and what can be done about it – alongside some highly charged themes around who is to 'blame'. This can be seen, for example, in the way that child sexual exploitation has been co-opted to make racist political points that play on the trope of the 'Muslim grooming gang' (Tufail, 2015; Cockbain, 2023). Therefore, while social care organisations are inherently engaged in an anxiety-provoking task when it comes to extra-familial risks and harms, the weight of uncertainty and unanswered questions about where the harm comes from and what can be done about it, married with the extremity of risk faced by young people transitioning into young adulthood, create a particularly turbulent field of anxiety, which is unique to this area of practice and research.

Returning to Menzies-Lyth's study, we might imagine that if offered emotional containment, the nurses could connect with depressive feelings related to the suffering and death of patients, and that, over time, the hospital systems would shift and the dysfunctional defences could be relinquished. However, it is harder to imagine an equivalent in the current context of young people affected by extra-familial risks or harms. Beyond taking a more realistic view of risk-taking and adolescent development, knowing what a depressive position would be is a challenge, as there should never be anything inevitable about a teenager being raped or stabbed. Similarly, looking at Cooper and Lees' (2015) study of a child safeguarding department, while familial harm is complex and subject to marketisation and extra-organisational pressures, there is nevertheless a well-established set of practices, policy frameworks, legal precedents, processes, expectations and partnerships that exist to provide some certainty and containment. The same cannot be said for harms beyond the home, making innovation in this area particularly affective and complex.

Uncertainty at the practice, policy and political levels creates an anxiety field underpinned by philosophical preoccupations about extra-familial risks and harms. Sitting largely at the unconscious level, these fundamental questions ask: 'What should we be doing?'; 'Why should we be doing it?'; 'Can we do it?'; 'Are we doing it right?'; 'How can we know if we are doing it right?'; and 'Is this really our work?'. The answers are not available – or available only in tentative and inconsistent forms. What makes this so problematic is the lack of spaces for voicing uncertainty. Instead, as we explored in Chapter Five, considerable work is directed towards avoiding these big, fundamental and unsettling questions, and the enormity of the culture and policy change that they demand. Perhaps this energy is unconsciously displaced into a feverish interest in knowledge acquisition towards needing to find things out: the listing of names, the mapping of peers, the giving of updates and intelligence. This is something we saw across the data set: a preoccupation with something being perpetually out of reach; something or someone being missing; some unobtainable knowledge that must be found; and a kind of magical belief that certainty and complete knowledge is the path to keeping young people safe. This, we argue, is an unconscious manifestation of a collective anxiety related to having such an uncertain task.

Institutional ethnography asks us to consider, 'In whose interest is this working?'. It seems to us that the defences described here are enacted to protect those at the forefront of practice from feeling the full force of the harm caused to young people and to protect organisations from having to face the uncertainty void that exists at the core of safeguarding work with young people beyond their homes. Ultimately, however, no one is served by these defence processes. If defences exist because they are necessary, the only way to reconnect with a more compassionate and less defensive set of practices is to render them redundant. Here, we return to the role of organisational containment. We argue that these data and analysis makes a strong case for emotional support for practitioners and managers to be a core part of all extra-familial work (and a core element of related research studies too). This is not an optional extra, just for those whose health and well-being is adversely impacted by the work. Rather, this should be understood as integral to the implementation of innovation in this field, as evidently necessary as wearing oven gloves to take something from a hot oven. We must take seriously the intolerable anxieties facing professionals doing this work and advocate for a thinking mind that can tolerate the uncertainty void at the core of this work. Particularly in the light of recent media discussions about the 'single-word inspections' in education undertaken by Ofsted and the impact that this can have on individual leaders, we argue for a compassionate appreciation of the complexity of the tasks involved in safeguarding young people from extra-familial risks and harms. As we approach innovation – particularly innovation in the area of adolescent safety and harm – our message is that we should do so with caution and care, and make provision for the inevitable uncertainty and turbulence that is associated with it. In this way, organisations will have a stronger chance of innovating in such a way that stays in touch with the needs of young people and partnering with them to find respectful, caring and humane routes to safety.

Conclusion

The story we have been telling in this chapter is about how new forms of high-risk and high-profile safeguarding work, subject to an inadequate policy, practice and legislative framework, have led to innovation characterised by defensive practice. To move forward, we need to acknowledge the anxiety-provoking context surrounding innovation in safeguarding responses to extra-familial risks and harms. If we do this, we will be in a stronger position to see the type of practice described in this chapter for what it is: urgent and pressured innovation activity that deflects the focus away from the lurking, big questions and intense feelings that high-risk work inevitably generates in an environment of uncertainty. Routinised practice, depersonalised ways of talking about young people and a preoccupation with information gathering and 'intelligence' all speak of organisational systems defending themselves against an untenable situation while needing to be seen to be doing something. When systems are thus defended, they can lose touch with their task – in this case, finding new ways to make life safer and better for young people. Rather than innovations in building relationships with young people and understanding their experiences as a foundation for this work, we often see innovations that seek new ways to find things out about young people, despite the lack of evidence that this leads to a safer or better life for them.

As we will explore further in Chapter Seven, organisational systems like this, subject to intense psychosocial anxieties, need reflective spaces. Those of us leading innovations in the fields of extra-familial risks and harms – whether in practice or in research roles – need to face up to the reality that this is an area of work beset with multidirectional anxieties. We need to cultivate self-awareness of how the uncertain conditions of innovation impact us, and we ignore this at our peril. From direct practice through to senior management level, innovators in the field of extra-familial risks and harms need to carve out emotionally containing spaces, where the complexity of the tasks we are involved in can be spoken about and their impact explored (Baldwin, 2008; McPheat and Butler, 2014). It is our ethical imperative to prioritise facing these things honestly together. Only in this way can we create better innovation conditions that allow us to move beyond defensive practices and towards organisational systems characterised by relationships, care and respect for young people.

Key chapter insights into policy and practice

- Practice in the field of extra-familial risks and harms is emotionally demanding, high risk and anxiety provoking.
- Innovation in this field is complex and uncertain due to limitations in national policy, legislation and practice guidance.
- The sense of urgency and pressure to reform and transform services that this combination creates may mean the need for emotionally containing and reflective spaces to consider unsettling feelings and fundamental questions is overlooked, and defensive practice ensues, characterised by routinised activity, depersonalised ways of talking about young people and a preoccupation with information gathering and 'intelligence'.
- To address this at an organisational level, the complex and demanding nature of this field needs to be acknowledged, and reflective spaces providing emotional containment should be prioritised.
- Containment also needs to be provided at a macro-level by the provision of a coherent and settled policy context and sufficiently resourced services.

SEVEN

Building learning partnerships between innovators and researchers

Introduction

In this penultimate chapter, we move in a slightly different direction to explore our distinctive approach to building innovator–researcher relationships. Positioning this relationship as a partnership aligns with and complements the emphasis in Chapter Two of innovation activities being a collaborative endeavour involving all stakeholders in every stage of the innovation cycle. To better understand the intricacies of this relationship, we begin the chapter by outlining three generative and compatible conceptual frames – learning partnerships, para-ethnography and the analytic third – and move on to apply these ideas by drawing on data generated from within our six case-study sites and from our Learning and Development Network activities. The chapter concludes by summarising the affordances of these collaborations in professional practice in sites of innovation in the field of social care.

Three generative conceptual frames

Understanding the characteristics of learning partnerships

Originating in the context of public policy, consultancy learning partnerships are characterised by a commitment to equalising power and authority that is built on shared trust between the respective partners. In its re-imaginings of more effective forms of government, the Centre for Public Impact proposes a learning partner to be 'an organization that helps others build their own capacity to learn', placing an emphasis on 'sensemaking': 'Sensemaking is about creating space for listening, reflection and the exploration of meaning beyond the usual boundaries, allowing different framings, stories and viewpoints to be shared and collectively explored' (Centre for Public Impact, 2021). The attraction of a sensemaking approach for our research is its investment in developing 'mindsets, culture, capabilities, and tools that will enable them [our case-study sites] to commit to a process of continuous experimentation and learning' (Centre for Public Impact, 2021). This rationale aligns with our interest in understanding how welfare organisations make sense of, and respond to, the complexities of innovation processes and practice (Lowe and French, 2021). Our interest was also sparked by our research team members – Research in Practice and Innovation Unit – who have particular expertise in creating learning partnerships. For Research in Practice, the role of a learning partnership 'was not to undertake an evaluation, but rather to enable and support the exploration of emerging themes and send reflections at various points in the Programme's journey' (Godar and Botcherby, 2021: 3). Central to the understanding of the learning-partner role are: (1) a shared, collaborative partnership rather than a model of an 'expert' or 'objective' consultant maintaining a distance from the client; (2) learning that takes place in the midst of action rather than being delivered at the end of a project; and (3) an approach with swift feedback loops so that changes can be made 'in real time'.

Para-ethnography

Historically, research relationships in ethnography were framed in such a way that researchers were conceived as having a degree of 'power over' the 'relatively powerless other' being studied – 'the power to document, to classify, and to categorize' (Archer and Souleles, 2021: 195–6). Para-ethnography seeks to challenge this established orthodoxy and redistribute the power flow by designing organisational ethnographies that are conducted in a 'side-by-side way' with a 'quasi-peer relationship between organizational scholars and internal analysts' (Islam, 2015: 232). To achieve this, para-ethnography seeks to emphasise the reciprocity between the researchers, who often have professional identifications with, but are external to, the spaces they are researching, and the internally situated research participants, who, through their innovative work, are often engaged in research-aligned activities. Islam (2015: 232) outlines how '[a]s a result of these dual processes, organisational ethnographers may be increasingly indistinguishable from those they study'. Holmes and Marcus (2008: 232), who coined the term para-ethnography, also recognise this challenge: 'How do we pursue our inquiry when our subjects are themselves engaged in intellectual labors that resemble approximately or are entirely indistinguishable from our own methodological practices?' Although the language used by Holmes and Marcus (2008) in their definition of para-ethnography is somewhat problematic (specifically, where they refer to those being researched as 'subjects'), as it does not fully acknowledge the shared power and equal status inherent in this approach, their question offers a helpful provocation. Para-ethnography provides a helpful understanding the learning partnerships we established, which brought us together as equal collaborators on a shared endeavour with distinctive, but compatible, roles and agendas.

The analytic third

Our experience of engaging in learning partnerships across the Innovate Project underlined for us that the emotional impact of innovation work in the welfare sphere and the defences it generates are both under-identified and insufficiently conceptualised. In light of our growing awareness of the significance of these psychosocial dynamics (see Chapters 5 and 6), the psychoanalytic concept of the 'analytic third' has helped us to make sense of how learning partnerships can enhance understanding of what helps and hinders progress in innovation spaces. According to Diamond (2007: 142): 'The analytic third is what we create when we make genuine contact with one another at a deeper emotional level of experience whether in dyads, groups, communities, organizations.' A key feature of the analytic third is its capacity to facilitate a triadic perspective of being observed, being an observer and observing oneself. In line with this characteristic, learning partnerships and para-ethnography also recognise how the dynamic positioning of the self in relation to itself and others allow for the 'found imaginaries' (Rabinow et al, 2008: 70) of critical knowledges produced through fieldwork to emerge.

Learning through regular meetings

From the beginning of our relationships with our case-study sites, the researchers in each of the three Innovate Project research strands (Contextual Safeguarding, Transitional Safeguarding and Trauma-informed Practice) established a pattern of regular meetings with their key contact(s) in each site. Of particular significance for these meetings was the impact of the global COVID-19 pandemic, which extended across the majority of the fieldwork phase of the Innovate

Project. While it is hard to say categorically, it is likely that our commitment to these regular meetings was heightened by the pandemic's impact, as we were more mindful of how important it was to establish and maintain positive and productive virtual relationships in the absence of opportunities to meet in person. In some of our sites, we were able to meet in person with our key research partners towards the end of our fieldwork stage and spend time with them in their locality. This was a rewarding experience and an important reminder of the effort needed to build and maintain trusting relationships in an almost exclusively virtual space.

Over time, it became apparent that the regular meetings served a range of purposes: (1) enabling the research team to be updated on developments and kept abreast of how the innovation work was progressing; (2) allowing researchers to be inquisitive and to express curiosity about innovation activities, barriers and enablers; and (3) providing opportunities for sites to draw on our wider knowledge of innovation in this sector and emergent learning derived from the fieldwork. Essentially, the meetings involved a dialogue that helped both us, as the researchers, and the site contacts, as the innovators, to collaboratively reflect on, and take stock of, what was happening. The emphasis of learning partnerships and para-ethnography on collaborative and mutual learning meant that intrinsic to these relationships was an understanding that, as researchers, it was neither appropriate nor possible for us to position ourselves as either 'independent' or 'objective'. Rather, these approaches encourage relationships to develop that are characterised by interdependence and intersubjectivity with informants involved, 'not only in data gathering, but also in interpretive process, collaborative critical reflexivity' (Islam, 2015: 236).

A matter of reliability and trust

A striking aspect of these regular meetings was the value our site partners placed on the sense of stability and continuity that they generated. This was in stark contrast to the widespread experience of workforce 'churn' in the sector and the inevitable disruptions – senior leadership changes, organisational realignments and shifting welfare priorities – that arose across the two years in which we were engaged with the sites. For example, over the course of our research, one project manager involved with the innovation work reported to three different senior leaders and experienced periods of time when he was without a named line manager.

Our learning partners placed particular value on our ongoing presence in their organisations when the innovation activities or engagement with the processes associated with innovation slowed, stalled or even floundered:

> 'I think it's been nice to have that opportunity to, kind of, think through some ideas, but, actually, I do think it has been valuable in pushing forward certain things. So, again, from my perspective, I have really valued it, even though I've moaned continuously to you all. ... I do think there is a level that, had we not had your support, it probably would have crashed and burnt even sooner than it has.' (Local innovation lead)

The meeting space served as 'a constant', and even when it felt as if there was little to report, discussions remained lively and purposeful. Periods of lesser activity can represent a 'risk point' on innovation journeys, where momentum may be lost (Godar and Botcherby, 2021), and the continuous pattern of our meetings appeared to play an important role in keeping issues alive and 'on the agenda'. This was especially pertinent when our key site partners were not members of the local senior leadership teams. It allowed them to use the outcomes of our discussions as a vehicle for keeping the people who were ultimately responsible for the innovation actively engaged.

In contrast to the regularity and reliability of these meeting spaces, the meeting structure was intentionally looser and more fluid, enabling the meetings to be responsive to the needs of the research sites at particular points in time. Our role as ethnographers with an interest in social care innovation more broadly, rather than as evaluators who were focused on the effectiveness of the sites' specific innovations per se, also helped to establish our benign neutrality, akin to a 'critical friend'. This was vividly described by one local leader as us embodying an "inquisitive, not inquisitional", approach. This enabled our learning partners to experience the research as a non-threatening, generative activity that allowed them to learn about: (1) their own organisation's idiosyncrasies; (2) features of their site-specific innovation journeys; and (3) their individual responses to the challenges faced by young people experiencing extra-familial risks and harms in their specific localities.

The loose definition and structure of these meetings was underpinned by an understanding that the space was shared equally, with both the research teams and site partners bringing information, updates or queries. As the researchers, we would pose questions and offer insights or reflections in response to site updates on activities. Discussions incorporated theoretical or empirical knowledge and wider contextual issues (emotional, social and political) that expanded the understanding or scope of innovation. The conversations that developed invariably focused on the complexities of the innovation journey, which have been reflected on throughout this book. Rather than resulting in defined action plans, however, discussions concluded naturally, allowing all of us to retain our distinct roles as researchers or innovators. Each partner took away insights, and actions were progressed independently or together, as appropriate, in relation to our specific research or innovation agendas. For us, as researchers, the discussion might organically lead to the identification of a previously unknown professional, team or service within the organisation that it was appropriate for us to engage with. As innovators, our research partners could find that the conversation triggered a thought about how to address an aspect of the innovation that they felt had got stuck or that had not occurred to them. These fascinating dynamics are at the heart of para-ethnographic approaches, where 'researchers note their occasional insightful leaps of imagination, but also their self-serving biases and their moments of ingenuousness and learn about their own project in the process. Thus, para-ethnography involves a mirroring of ethnographer and informant roles, as these roles interpenetrate each other' (Islam, 2015: 238).

In the sites where an open and responsive attitude came to characterise these meetings, a sense of trust was fostered that helped mitigate the ever-present possibility that the sites might feel 'done to' or positioned as 'an object of enquiry' by the research process. This type of relationship was in stark contrast, we realised, to most local authorities' experiences of the relationships associated with inspection regimes and external evaluations, which invariably operate somewhat covertly, only sharing outcomes on completion of the exercise. Given how widespread these practices have become in the public sector, local authorities have become familiar with these dynamics and developed their own strategies for managing them. The principles informing para-ethnography recognise the 'hybridity, institutional complexity, and discursive struggles' (Islam, 2015: 244) that characterise contemporary organisations, and this realisation further underlined for us the importance of establishing reciprocal learning partnerships. One of our sites had faced significant organisational and system-wide difficulties in progressing their innovation plans. The fact that they were willing to meet with us at the end of the fieldwork phase to undertake a journey-mapping exercise suggests that they had experienced us as sufficiently embodying the respectful and non-judgemental principles of para-ethnography and learning partnerships to feel safe doing so.

A matter of reciprocity

In addition to these regular meeting spaces supporting innovation activity, our learning partners also acknowledged their contribution to promoting the well-being of the professionals engaged in the work. In one site engaged in trauma-informed innovation, the learning partners explicitly acknowledged how the regular meetings with the researchers were "like having therapy" or like a "proper" form of supervision, as their current supervision experiences were not deemed to be fit for purpose. One of our Transitional Safeguarding site partners said that they "got what they needed" from the meetings and felt that the strategic leaders driving the innovation would also have benefited from participating in these regular sessions, described as spaces to think, to "horizon-scan" and to develop the "best way to build this approach". The mutuality of this was explicitly named by another Transitional Safeguarding partner:

'So, no, I think from our side it is … I think it's been really helpful, and I've really enjoyed working with you both, but also just … it's just thinking about how I can improve things and reframing how I would do certain things and learning. I just feel like it's been a really kind of … from my side, I've also benefited from the learning there as well, and so I don't want it … it feels like it's been … I hope it's been mutually beneficial for you as well.'

Throughout more than two years of engagement with our sites, we sought to be continuously vigilant about our positioning, that is, 'Not assuming participants to be insiders, and the ethnographers, outsiders' (Islam, 2015: 241). The status of the research strand teams as independent from professional practice and leadership enabled site staff to utilise our insights or observations as leverage to influence and energise their innovation journey. The periodic internal reports we produced for each site at key time points across the project were experienced as particularly beneficial, as they provided content for the sites to reflect on, assisted them in developing their thinking and informed next steps in the innovation process. These regular forms of information sharing served to maintain a transparent engagement with our learning partners, creating a genuine sense of mutual exchange, and helped to avoid the research being caught in unhelpful protracted time frames, whereby sites did not hear about the research findings until a full analysis of the data had been completed. The provision of feedback and findings in 'real time' proved key to the sites being able to use the information provided to positively influence their innovation processes, including to argue for increased resources. As the following excerpt from a journey-mapping exercise with one of our Transitional Safeguarding sites illustrates, our interim report was used by the site to draw attention to the persistent lack of engagement by one part of the system. The intervention proved to be successful in securing greater buy-in across their system, which has been maintained:

> 'I think the thing that, sort of, helped that pick-up was whether I should have done this or not. I don't know how you guys would feel about this, but the report that you produced for the end of Phase 1 report, we kind of … used as a bit of a lever. I very much used it as a bit of a lever.' (Local innovation leader)

Our experience of conducting the regular meetings was what particularly drew our attention to how the concept of the analytic third helps to explain the dynamics of learning partnerships. Through our collaborative relationship, our partners were able to adopt an observational stance on their own innovation work, and we were allowed to observe how they engaged in this space with each other, as colleagues, and with us, as researchers. These reciprocal observational positions allowed for new perspectives and ideas to emerge. Evidence of this arose when the lead contact in one of our Transitional Safeguarding sites informed us during one of our regular meetings that the plan to introduce a new children's services panel that would assess vulnerable young people requiring a Transitional Safeguarding response had been revoked. Instead, a decision had been reached to amalgamate a Transitional Safeguarding assessment activity into an existing multi-agency adult services panel. Conversations with us in our regular meetings had explored the value of new panels, and we were struck by how the site's new-found insight into the limitations of conventional responses to persistent challenges – that is, the creation of a new panel – appeared to have exerted some influence over them identifying a different approach. This change of perspective allowed the organisation to abandon what could be seen as a defensive response that stayed with what was familiar in favour of something innovative and new. While we cannot definitely claim that this decision was influenced by their engagement with us, it appears that the new insights that emerged might, in part, have been attributable to the relationship with us, leading to a confidence to let go of unconscious defences to innovation (see Chapter Six).

For the research team, the mutuality and reciprocity built into the learning partnership model enabled us to benefit from the rich discussion available through the regular meetings and gain in-depth understanding of the 'on the ground', 'in real time', everyday nature of innovation. Throughout the project, the research team worked together in our own reflective forums, where we shared research data, such as an interview excerpt or ethnographic observation notes, and explored our reactions to the material. As a consequence, we were able to reflect on our own conduct, as well as that of the organisations we were collaborating with, and recognise, as the analytic third conceptualises it, 'the psychological (triangular) space between self and other, subject and object, fantasy and reality – the third dimension that emerges from two persons fully engaged in the exploration of unconscious meanings, reasons, motives and actions' (Diamond, 2007: 142). Holding this perspective helped us to avoid jumping to conclusions or making assumptions about what we were seeing and hearing, and facilitated a more trustworthy and authentic analytic engagement with the data.

Learning through journey mapping

Journey mapping, derived from the world of social consultancy, seeks to capture the process that an organisation has undertaken to develop an aspect of a service or a system (Oeij et al, 2019). As part of the Transitional Safeguarding strand's work with a wider group of local authorities who were involved in our Learning and Development Network, members were invited to take part in a journey-mapping exercise, where they could reflect on the process and progress of their innovation activities. Members of the research team facilitated the exercise and paid particular attention to the relational and emotional dimensions of the journey, with specific reference to the key 'pain points' or opportune moments that the sites could identify, and the emotions they evoked. In the process of conducting the mapping exercise and the follow-up conversations with our learning partners, several common experiences emerged.

A matter of feeling

One innovation leader described the journey-mapping process it as a "cathartic" experience. The tone of the comment indicated that this realisation had come as something of a surprise. For another site lead, recalling the circumstances of the vulnerable young woman that had triggered their organisation's Transitional Safeguarding work, and the subsequent challenges they had encountered along the way, was emotionally overwhelming:

> 'I'm quite happy to share why I'm crying … I loved it, as hard as it was, and by God, some of it was so hard [crying] in some ways, I feel a fraud talking about, "Oh,

didn't we do". And we tried really hard, and I think some things we did do well. But I come down to [crying] some of the people I still feel we failed, and I don't like that.' (Site lead)

In seeking to account for her response, this site lead articulated how unusual it was to review the work she had been leading through "an emotional lens", reflecting that their main focus was always on "doing" and not on "being". She went on to reflect on the emotional toll of the work and the energy she put into providing emotional support for the staff for whom she had management responsibility. This reverberated for us as a research team, as we had noted that a number of professionals in our sites referred to their 'passion' for Transitional Safeguarding when describing their connection to this work. In some instances, the passion was closely connected with a professional's personal identification or experience:

'I genuinely believe in [Transitional Safeguarding], not only because I see what it potentially could do, but actually as a young adult … there were times where I was sitting in this space and arena, and years ago, we didn't have this, but if we had have done, if I was a young adult now, I'd be in your cohort.' (Transitional Safeguarding lead)

For others, it connected to having their own children who were approaching, or in, this transitional space. In such instances, it was clear that the work touched a deeply personal chord and that the mutuality and trust that were integral to our learning partnerships enabled the emotional dimensions of the work to be expressed.

The explicit attention paid in the journey-mapping exercise to the emotional dimensions of innovation work highlighted the prevalence and impact of these aspects of daily practice, as well as the lack of attention they receive. We repeat here our conclusions from Chapters Five and Six: unless the emotional impact of this work is acknowledged by practitioners and responded to by senior leaders, it is highly likely that it will, in unconscious ways, impede the progress of innovation.

A matter of perspective

One interesting feature of the journey-mapping process that participants identified as helpful was the adoption of a retrospective lens. Looking backwards served the purpose of allowing the participants to see the whole journey to date and to recognise what they had achieved. This felt of particular significance, as we heard repeatedly how frustrated individuals were by what felt like *very* slow, incremental progress, or, to use the phrase of one site contact, "taking two steps forward and one back" – very much in line with the recursive nature of the stages of innovation that we alluded to in Chapters Two and Three. There was evidence that the thinking of individuals undertaking the mapping exercise was dominated by prospective mindsets and a preoccupation with forward planning, which could prevent them from maintaining an accurate view of what had already been achieved. Indeed, for the Transitional Safeguarding innovation with the "two steps forward and one back" experience, the combination of us facilitating a review workshop with a range of Transitional Safeguarding partners and, subsequently, completing a journey-mapping exercise with our two main contacts from this site had significant ramifications: first, it contributed to the recognition that expectations about what is a realistic pace of change needed to be radically revised; and, second, it helped inform a successful funding request to enable the local area to adopt a more accurate, and hopefully more effective, timeline for the innovation process to unfold over.

Inevitably, innovation projects do not always go to plan, and for one of our Transitional Safeguarding sites, the progress made in the course of our involvement with them had stalled. Despite these circumstances, in the context of a journey-mapping exercise, it was heartening to hear the senior leader able to express her disappointment at not having made more progress and simultaneously maintain a realistic perspective, seeing it not as a failure but as an integral part of the iterative and recursive innovation process, as outlined in Chapter Three.

Conclusion

In this chapter, we have explored how the reconfiguration of ethnographic research relationships as learning partnerships has the potential to maximise the learning for all the parties involved. Drawing on the insights afforded by para-ethnography and the analytic third, innovators can gain new perspectives on their specific circumstances, and as a consequence, it is likely that their innovation activities will be more responsive and attuned to the context in which they are located. Our journey as a research team through these innovation landscapes has led us to experience unexpected encounters and expanded our theoretical and conceptual horizons. These, in turn, have triggered meaningful insights – the 'found imaginaries' referred to earlier – both for us as researchers and, in the spirit of the partnership-working practice we established, for our site contacts, the innovators.

Key chapter insights for policy and practice

- Risks and barriers to progress are ever present in innovation contexts and must be recognised and worked with.
- Learning partnerships can encourage attention to the impact of emotions and defensive dynamics in innovation spaces, helping to minimise their potentially adverse impact on process and progress, and maximising the likelihood of positive outcomes.
- The establishment of effective and collaborative learning partnerships requires an inclusive, non-hierarchical attitude of 'equal but different'

from the outset to ensure all project stakeholders start on the same footing.

- Researchers need to cycle fluidly between an observing 'outsider' stance (primarily reflecting and noticing what is happening, and how things change over time) and a more involved semi-insider position (sharing insights that could generate reflexivity and change for the sites), all the while relating to the sites as active, equal partners.

EIGHT

Implications of this study for policy and practice

Introduction

This book has considered three interrelated domains: (1) the conditions that facilitate, rather than impede, innovation in social care and related settings; (2) the specific factors and processes relevant to innovation in the field of extra-familial risks and harms; and (3) the characteristics of Contextual Safeguarding, Trauma-informed Practice and Transitional Safeguarding as innovation frameworks, and what they demand in adoption and implementation. In this final chapter, we step back from the detailed scrutiny of different aspects of our fieldwork and the insights it has generated to consider the overarching themes that have emerged across our diverse research sites and wider project activities. We reference those themes that support and align with existing literature and those that offer new insights into innovation practices, suggesting some ways in which innovation in this field might be progressed. However, rather than concluding the book with an itemised list of recommendations of 'how to innovate in social care', we refer readers back to Chapter Two, which sets out the foundational contextual domains that may facilitate or impede innovation, and offers insights into how they should be taken into account through the innovation journey. Instead, in this chapter, we offer critical reflections, queries and provocations for innovators and policy makers before summarising some key implications for innovation policy and practice in this field.

While our fieldwork took place in the UK and we have referred many times throughout this book to the UK policy and practice context, many of the more general insights regarding innovation made within this chapter have relevance for practice improvement and system change in other countries in the Global North with a similar conception of social work, social care and child welfare. We specify where we think our insights apply primarily to the UK and couch the whole discussion within the caution offered by our most strongly emphasised point made in this book: context matters when innovating and adopting approaches trialled elsewhere – and it matters whether that be at the local level, cross-nationally or across country borders.

Key questions for social care innovation in the field of extra-familial risks and harms

Is innovation the right way to proceed?

Innovation is a field of activity that involves radically different ways of thinking and acting compared to the status quo but that also needs to balance paradigm and system transformation with ethical concerns in order to mitigate against any potentially negative unforeseen consequences that disrupting services for vulnerable people may entail (Hampson et al, 2021; see also Chapters Five and Six). This is important in social care generally but particularly so in systems and interventions for young people affected by extra-familial risks and harms given the delicate balancing of risk, care, rights, voice and autonomy that is involved (Firmin et al, 2022). As such, innovation is situated in the liminal and interstitial spaces between continuity and change, connection and disruption, and the micro-level of seemingly small changes to everyday practice and the macro-level of large-scale systems change. In complexity theory terms, this position is described as the 'edge of chaos' (Hudson, 2000), characterised by maximal creativity and capacity for problem solving.

The critical 'troubling' of taken-for-granted assumptions at the start of the innovation journey that can be facilitated by these conditions includes querying not only whether existing practices and systems meet the needs and rights of young people, families and communities but also whether innovation is likely to provide the hoped-for benefits and improvements. Both as a first step before embarking on innovation projects and as an ongoing frame for critical reflexivity, innovators should consider the following questions: 'Can innovation solve the "problems" it is intended to address?'; and 'Is it possible for innovation to succeed against the structural "odds" that may impede new practice systems or methods flourishing and sustaining over time?' (Hampson et al, 2021). As we discussed in Chapters Two, Three and Four, innovation may well be necessary to find new and more effective ways of responding to young people affected by extra-familial risks and harms because current systems often undermine more incremental approaches to practice improvement. In the case of Trauma-informed Practice (see Chapter Four), for example, it transpired that individual practitioners struggled to sustain new learning about this practice framework unless it was reinforced by higher-order system transformation regarding supervision, workloads and emotional containment.

Innovation also provokes and sanctions the unsettling of existing paradigms and the co-production of rights-based, youth-centred, relationship-based ways of seeing and responding to young people (Hampson et al, 2021). As we also noted with our previous evidence review (Firmin et al, 2022), where attempts are made to introduce such new ways of thinking, being and doing by 'tinkering' with existing systems, such as through a distributed programme of training, it is much harder for new principles and methods to gain traction; the old patterns, such as responsibilising, individualising and pathologising cultures, are more likely to seep back in, and this undermines the aims of even potentially transformational new frameworks.

It was clear that local innovation, too, is limited in its capacity to address the macro-systems within which it is rooted, such as the social conditions that provoke or intensify contextual risks to young people, for example, poverty, racism and marginalising educational systems (Billingham and Irwin-Rogers, 2022). Perhaps only a more radical dismantling and rebuilding of these wider social structures may be capable of promoting social justice, such as those suggested by contemporary 'abolitionist' perspectives in the US, which are focused not only on dismantling but also on radically rebuilding structures to move from surveillance, separation and punishment towards community-embedded support (Dettlaff et al, 2020). It was notable that our Scottish local authority site operated under the devolved government's policy 'Promise' that 'All children in Scotland's "care system" will have a good, loving childhood. They will feel loved. They will have their needs met. And they will have their rights upheld' (The Promise, Scotland, 2020). This 'ruling relation' (Smith, 2005: 51) at a policy level had (in our view) enabled Scottish practitioners to much more readily build relational and trauma-informed practices with children and young people, rooted in empathic and critical understandings of their life experiences, social contexts and expressed wishes, than their counterparts in English statutory settings.

The intellectual rigour and emotional stress of the 'risky' creative experimentation entailed with frameworks that require adaptation are, of course, not inconsiderable. Innovation requires a capacity for tolerating the uncertainty and potential anxieties brought about by the positions of liminality that the transition from the status quo to newly configured practices, services or systems inevitably involves. With reference to the principles of reflexivity, inquisitiveness and ongoing learning that we have discussed throughout this book, we emphasise again the importance of senior leaders providing system containment and embodying reflexivity. This should better enable staff to 'sit with "not knowing" and to maintain open-mindedness and curiosity' in conditions of uncertainty (Huegler and Ruch, 2022: 34).

Is there a good enough fit between model and context?

This unsettling, often disruptive, nature of innovation means that it is not always the best way of responding to an identified practice or system limitation. The anxiety it may provoke (see Chapter Six), the (often costly) operational capabilities it requires (see Chapter Two), its lengthy timescales for implementation and embedding, and the uncertainty of its outcomes (see Chapter Six) are not always well suited to cash-strapped statutory organisations or systems, with high staff turnover and a responsibility towards some of the most vulnerable and marginalised members of society. Perhaps, in these contexts, maintaining continuity is already a major challenge for systems and services, and so incremental improvements that do not stress the system and that enable existing commitments to be maintained might be a better approach. Fieldwork in our trauma-informed sites (see Chapter Four) suggests that it may be possible to move beyond viewing innovation and improvement as binary opposites, and to instead employ more modest, lower-cost processes of practice improvement to scaffold the early stages of development until some evidence of the beneficial nature of a new practice framework emerges; such evidence can then be used to build a case for the increased resources needed for more radical change. From a complexity theory perspective, starting with small-scale initiatives does not preclude the emergence of more widespread change across a system.

There may be a danger that dwelling on whether innovation is the 'right' approach could lead to increased risk aversion;

new ideas and initiatives may be stifled where the thought of attempting to depart from the status quo is considered too cumbersome and unlikely to lead to 'real' change. Acknowledging feelings of ambivalence or even emotional oscillation between pessimism and optimism vis-à-vis an organisation's or system's capacity to transform cultures and structures could be particularly important in the early stages of innovation endeavours. The degree to which those leading systems and enacting governance provide a containing and permissive environment within which creativity and defensible risk-taking is possible will be significant here (Lefevre et al, forthcoming). As discussed in Chapters Two and Three, innovation by necessity involves iterative experimentation with recursive learning loops. If these are seen as wasteful of time and money, then the temptation could be to push on regardless of indicators that a new approach is unlikely to yield fruit. Indeed, there will be little encouragement to take the leap into the unknown in the first place.

The 'dynamic tension' between 'fidelity and fit' must also be carefully considered when innovation models or frameworks are introduced to new settings (Castro et al, 2004: 41). The dominant diffusion approach in social innovation of adopting, with fidelity, manualised models or prescriptive instructions about systems or interventions that were birthed and shown to 'work' elsewhere (Rogers, 2003) may seem like a lower-risk approach to evidence-based practice, but the appropriateness of a template model for a new and very different context is not a given (Castro et al, 2004). Transfer of models between countries, particularly cross-continent, is likely to be complex given that policy and legislation governing practice diverge markedly across borders and evidence regarding cross-cultural adaption is fairly sparse (Brown, 2021). However, transfer is also challenging within countries given that there is often substantial demographic, economic and political diversity across regions (Castro et al, 2010). This was a key reason that our Innovate Project selected three frameworks that themselves required innovation and system configuration at a local level; we had deemed it both practical and ethical in the complex and rapidly evolving field of adolescent safeguarding, and in a context of constrained public spending, to ensure that new practice methods and systems were carefully tailored not only to national policy and legislative frameworks but also to local needs, operational capabilities and governance.

Is the groundwork for innovation in place?

Our fieldwork supported what the social innovation literature indicates: triggers and events that stimulate innovation, as well as the conditions that mobilise it, are crucial factors that influence the whole of the innovation journey, including design, embedding and scaling/spreading (Mulgan et al, 2007; Murray et al, 2010). An important dynamic in our sites and other organisations in the wider Learning and Development Network was whether innovation was perceived as forced upon public organisations through the insecurity and inadequacy of funding systems or whether it was seen genuinely as an 'option' with the potential to promote social justice agendas. While the very foundations of social care and the idea of innovation are based on ideas of 'making things better', it is essential that those involved critically interrogate the basis for such assumptions and any hidden purposes within innovation agendas rather than just 'performing to conform to narratives of success' – as we have discussed in Chapter Five of this book. This is particularly the case in contexts of neoliberalism and austerity, such as the UK (Jones, 2018), the Netherlands (Van der Pas and Jansen, forthcoming) and Portugal (Jesus and Amaro, forthcoming), where innovation has at times been criticised as seeking to compensate for the chronic underfunding of existing services or masking an agenda of privatisation. This raises the question as to whether innovation in such circumstances provides the freedom for public services to do things differently, including through radical transformation, or whether it exacerbates quasi-market competition and performance anxiety as well, particularly in countries like the UK, where regulatory oversight, performance rankings and a highly critical public discourse about social work loom large.

Although this was not particularly apparent in our study, it is entirely understandable in such circumstances that organisations, services or local areas may rebadge existing plans for system restructuring or the better implementation of existing frameworks as a way of attracting such resources. More problematic is where the only funding available is for innovation rather than other forms of practice improvement, which tempts services down the road to innovation without the ground having been adequately prepared. If demonstrating the will and capacity to innovate is a required condition, or ruling relation, for local leaders to keep up with the zeitgeist and acquire the resources they need to respond adequately to young people and their families, then there is more risk that performative approaches will dominate and that individual and organisational anxiety and other defences will be heightened.

The foundational contextual domains and their components, which we outlined in Chapter Two, as well as the accompanying set of reflective questions for each stage of the innovation journey provided there, offer a framework for determining whether the necessary conditions are present for innovation to flourish and sustain. We emphasise again that this reflective framework seeks to provide not a pro forma for success that can be replicated across contexts but, rather, a way for organisations and networks to examine what the prevailing conditions are over time and place, and to see how they might be made more optimal in each phase of innovation.

Are the right people on board?

In addition to (and perhaps more so than) the provision of appropriate organisational resources, it is people and their relationships that create a conducive context for innovation.

What we observed in our case-study sites corresponded strongly with what has been noted in the literature: innovation is mobilised by those with the creativity and verve to envisage a better future and drive it forward, but they need to work closely with others, such as data specialists and practitioners, to build the evidence for a compelling initial case. Buy-in is then more likely from the authorising environment (Moore, 2013): those senior leaders in local government who have the power and influence to sanction and resource change at each stage of innovation and if/when external conditions change. The imposition of top-down ideas is unlikely to gain traction unless practitioners are fully on board, so 'cheerleaders' are then needed to win hearts and minds at every level of the service, particularly at difficult moments when momentum might falter, and to provide the embodied knowledge to translate complex ideas into everyday tools and practices.

Given the interdependent nature and distributed power within social care systems, innovation that is more collaboratively produced, 'owned' and shaped is more likely to embed and sustain. Therefore, for new systems and interventions to have the best chance of working well and being responsive to the needs and preferences of those for whom the service is designed, collaboration and co-production with key stakeholders, including young people, families and communities, must be a central feature from the start. It was this final element that we saw to be most challenging for the sites that we worked with. As yet, the involvement of young people, in particular, as well as parents to a certain degree, in innovation design and its review remains at a very limited level – and this is reflected in the wider literature (see, for example, Bovarnick et al, 2018). We do not want to downplay the challenging nature of co-production with young people who could be considered some of the most marginalised within our society; as researchers, we too have struggled at times to achieve the meaningful participation of young people affected by extra-familial risks and harms. However, naming the challenge does not sanction our limitations. Unless and until co-production with young people is recognised as being central to the ethical legitimacy and effectiveness of an innovation and this commitment is concretised in actual time and resources, then it is likely that innovators and researchers will remain stuck in a cycle of, at best, only performatively engaging in participation activities and, at worst, continuing to responsibilise young people for being 'difficult to engage' when these activities do not bear fruit.

Collaborative approaches also mitigate against tendencies to place responsibility for the work involved in innovation projects (and the blame for perceived 'failures') in single leader figures – some of whom (as we saw) may in fact only have limited positional power within organisational and system hierarchies. If vision, direction, culture, enthusiasm and institutional knowledge rest solely with one or two key individuals, this may jeopardise the sustainability of innovation projects if they leave their role, particularly where this is due to pressures associated with this responsibility. As we highlighted in Chapters Five and Seven, adopting more collaborative approaches to innovation work is also likely to promote more realistic perspectives regarding the political, societal and structural levers and barriers at both national and local levels. With respect to services in the field of extra-familial risks and harms, these include: (1) decades of low prioritisation of universal services for young people, particularly in poorer and more marginalised communities; (2) the eroding of youth work and other more preventative social care infrastructures in many areas through years of austerity; and (3) ambivalent (or sometimes hostile) public attitudes towards some young people, particularly where they have been perceived as 'antisocial' or involved in criminality and are seen primarily as presenting a risk to others rather than being at risk of harm themselves (Hanson and Holmes, 2014; Billingham and Irwin-Rogers, 2022).

Given this premise for collaborative approaches and given the unpredictability, distributed power and uncertainty in the complex systems that co-production involves, what, then, should leadership roles entail? Above all, it is incumbent on leaders to create and maintain a climate of curiosity, flexibility, reflexivity and adaptability, in which anxiety is acknowledged and contained, and the importance of learning through experience is foregrounded (Baldwin, 2008; McPheat and Butler, 2014; see also Chapter Five). Such a climate provides permission for a range of positive and negative feelings and views about innovation to come to the fore throughout the process, for energy and hope to rise or flatten, and for productive struggles and challenges to be surfaced and worked with. The capacity to achieve orderly implementation or predictable targets may then become secondary to the ability to navigate complexity and unpredictability given the 'edge of chaos' contexts and complex adaptive systems of many innovation projects (see Chapter Three), which may mean that they 'can only be steered, rather than controlled' (Smith, 2019: 427), via processes of system stewardship (Lowe and French, 2021).

Are expectations realistic?

We return to the image of ecocycles introduced in Chapter Three to emphasise the organic time frames, slow speed and recursive characteristics that innovation in social care is likely to entail. Developing a realistic understanding of the slow growth of innovation processes and the delicacy of the conditions needed for them to take root may be one of the most important ways of managing expectations. This includes looking forward as well as backwards, taking time for planning, implementing, reviewing and integrating innovations, sanctioning and resourcing iterative development, and allowing innovations the necessary time to embed and flourish before they are expected to produce the intended beneficial outcomes for professionals, young people, families and communities alike. Unfortunately, expectations of commissioners, funders, evaluators, practitioners, leaders and young people and their families and communities may not always be realistic and attuned to these processes and timescales. Despite the fieldwork and analysis phase of our own project having a longer than usual funding time frame (2.5 years), this has not allowed us to see any of the innovation projects in our sites reach a stage where they were considered 'fully' embedded and finalised. Adequate time and funding for innovations to unfold and for longitudinal research follow-up should, then, be another priority for the sector.

As we outlined in Chapter Two, innovation involves a multitude of contextual factors, many of which may not be in the control of individuals or even collaborative leader/ stewardship collectives, relying as they do, instead, on the intricate interactions between team or family microsystems. The individual elements of these microsystems may include: (1) the capabilities, cultures and climates of organisations and communities (mesosystems); (2) the inter-organisational systems at local levels (exosystems); and (3) the macrosystems of law and policy. This complexity may give rise to a wide range of possible directions and iterations throughout the lifespan of an innovation project. As we discussed in Chapter Three, this may include recursiveness – pausing, potentially faltering and a later return to ideas and activities. Rather than a climate of judgement, shaming, fear and risk aversion, innovators need sanction to retreat to, and potentially recover from, phases of stagnation or decline, along with the permission to end the innovation work if ultimate success looks less likely or the personal or collective cost in terms of emotional labour and other demands becomes too high.

Do the three frameworks result in effective services or systems?

Here, we remind the reader that the intention of this book has not been to provide an evaluation of whether Trauma-informed Practice, Contextual Safeguarding and Transitional

Safeguarding might lead to effective services or systems, nor to extend their underpinning theorisations. We have either published that work elsewhere (for example, Huegler and Ruch, 2022; Holmes, 2022; Firmin et al, forthcoming; Lefevre et al, 2023; Lloyd et al, 2023; Peace, forthcoming) or it remains ongoing. Rather, the primary role of the three frameworks in this volume was to provide containers within which situated innovation processes in the six case-study sites could be placed under the microscope. While there is no clear evidence as yet that these three frameworks create improved safety outcomes for young people (see Chapter One), we emphasise again the relative newness of their emergence and how long it can take for innovation projects to embed, change practices and result in improved outcomes at a child level. It is worth noting, however, that sufficient indicators exist of a positive direction of travel such that we encourage readers to not only engage with these frameworks as promising stimulators of practice improvement, organisational change or system innovation in response to extra-familial risks and harms but also to consider the messages and key principles they have the potential to convey and contribute to wider innovation practice and practice improvement in this field.

In none of the six case-study sites did an 'ideal' new system configuration emerge that suggested itself as worthy of forming a template for replication elsewhere. Even with Contextual Safeguarding, which offers a 'toolkit' of guidance and practice tools and has had the most formal trials, including in Tanzania and Germany (Wroe et al, 2023), it is clear that every new site will still need to interpret the principles of the framework to local needs, resources and partnership arrangements (Firmin and Lloyd, 2022; Lefevre et al, 2023). This is not surprising, as these three frameworks are specifically oriented around the importance of operationalising principles in ways that are tailored to a local context (see Boxes 1.1, 1.2 and 1.3 in Chapter One). We see this flexibility offered by all three frameworks as a positive rather than a shortcoming.

Moreover, we suggest that the three frameworks offer more than conceptual outlines and approaches to be interpreted, shaped and developed into local innovations. Rather, combined, their underlying key principles (shown in Figure 8.1) can also: facilitate innovation journeys that pay sufficient attention to contexts; prioritise the safety of, and relationships among, all involved; and appropriately consider the transitional needs and implications that emanate from the uncertainty and liminality that change processes bring about.

Conclusion

This book has described innovation experiences in our research partner sites through the metaphor of 'journeys' and has set out the liminal and emergent 'edge of chaos' spaces in which many innovation projects may be situated. These characteristics mean that innovations may encounter a range of challenges and contradictions. Complexity theory, psychosocial perspectives and human-centred principles can remind us to consider not only what separates ideas, emotions, systems or lived experiences but also what connects them. Practices that involve professionals across services and hierarchies, as well as young people, families and their communities coming together, exchanging perspectives and trying 'to walk in each other's shoes', seem essential for managing the uncertainty and transitions involved in departing from the status quo towards new ideas, concepts and systems.

Leaders and innovators in social care must prioritise young people's safety, well-being and rights, and avoid contributing to the adversities plaguing organisations, systems and the communities they seek to support, some of which include high staff turnover, pressure through inspection and 'performance ranking' regimes, and the devastating impact of serious harm and deaths of young people – along with the actual or perceived failures of professionals, services, policy makers and communities to prevent these. It is not difficult to appreciate

Figure 8.1: Principles to be considered when innovating to address extra-familial risks and harms

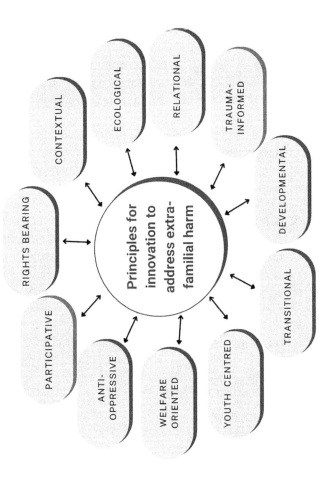

how these issues provide key rationales for innovating in the first place; however, they also highlight how such pressures may lead to innovation that is not always beneficial in its process or outcomes. Institutional ethnography has provided compelling insights into unhelpful or even abusive power structures, discourses and other ruling relations that may mean young people might be constrained, responsibilised, ignored or punished rather than listened to, respected, supported and enabled to flourish in the way that should be expected – and that professionals probably intend to enact, maybe even think they do.

It is important to stress that such principles as rights, youth-centredness, relationality, care, participation, choice, agency and respect require time, commitment, emotional containment and other conducive contextual factors (as summarised in Chapter Two and illustrated through this book). That our research has surfaced many unresolved issues, tensions and perhaps even contradictions in innovation processes, practices and contexts is not just incidental; rather, it is an expression of the complex, challenging and nuanced character of innovation in social care, particularly the field of extra-familial risks and harms. Above all, it points to learning as the main overall framework through which we – both innovators and researchers – can hope to hold on to, and make sense of, this complexity.

Key chapter insights for policy and practice

- The transformative, often disruptive, nature of innovation means that it is not always the best way of responding to an identified practice or system limitation.
- Drivers for innovation need to be critically interrogated to identify faulty assumptions and hidden motives and agendas, particularly where potential cost savings or access to additional resources are a draw.
- Discourses and power relations commonly govern the work of policy makers, system leaders and professionals in non-explicit and

unnoticed ways that need to be brought out into the open. Institutional ethnography offers a useful lens for such scrutiny.

- The risky and uncertain nature of innovation generates organisational and individual defences against anxiety. Psychosocial theories offer a window into understanding these and a framework for developing organisational containment and reflexivity.
- Such discourses and defences may mean that innovations are developed that prioritise child safeguarding and public protection concerns yet conflict with the rights, perspectives and wider welfare needs of young people. Co-production with young people is essential to ensure the ethical legitimacy and effectiveness of an innovation.
- Contextual Safeguarding, Trauma-informed Practice and Transitional Safeguarding continue to offer promise, but none of them can yet evidence their effectiveness in addressing extra-familial risks and harms. All three offer frameworks that require interpretation and operationalisation at a local level, enabling services and systems to be tailored for 'fit'.
- Policy makers, funders and leaders need to be aware that innovation is time-consuming and resource-intensive, involves repeated cycles of trialling and learning, and generally takes longer than expected. This should be taken into account in funding and evaluation timescales.

References

Aarons, G.A. and Palinkas, L.A. (2007) 'Implementation of evidence-based practice in child welfare: service provider perspectives', *Administration and Policy in Mental Health and Mental Health Services*, 34(4): 411–19.

Aarons, G.A., Hurlburt, M. and Horwitz S.M. (2011) 'Advancing a conceptual model of evidence-based practice implementation in public service sectors', *Administration and Policy in Mental Health and Mental Health Services*, 38(1): 4–23.

Accept Mission (2023) 'Improvement vs. innovation: defining the differences', 16 March. Available at: www.acceptmission.com/blog/improvement-vs-innovation/ (accessed 3 October 2023).

Archer, M. and Souleles, D. (2021) 'Introduction: ethnographies of power and the powerful', *Critique of Anthropology*, 41(3): 195–205.

Baldwin, M. (2008) 'Promoting and managing innovation: critical reflection, organizational learning and the development of innovative practice in a national children's voluntary organization', *Qualitative Social Work*, 7(3): 330–48.

Barrow Cadbury Commission (2005) *Lost in Transition: Report of the Barrow Cadbury Commission on Young Adults and the Criminal Justice System*. London: Barrow Cadbury Trust.

Bason, C. (2018) *Leading Public Sector Innovation: Co-creating for a Better Society* (2nd edn). Bristol: Policy Press.

Beckett, H. and Warrington, C. (2015) *Making Justice Work: Experiences of Criminal Justice for Children and Young People Affected by Sexual Exploitation as Victims and Witnesses*. Luton: University of Bedfordshire.

Billingham, L. and Irwin-Rogers, K. (2022) *Against Youth Violence: A Social Harm Perspective*. Bristol: Bristol University Press.

Bion, W.R. (1962) *Learning from Experience*. London: Heinemann.

Blase, K.A., Van Dyke, M., Fixsen, D.L. and Bailey, F.W. (2012) 'Implementation science: key concepts, themes, and evidence for practitioners in educational psychology', in B. Kelly and D.F. Perkins (eds) *Handbook of Implementation Science for Psychology in Education*. Cambridge: Cambridge University Press, pp 13–34.

Bloom, S.L. (2005) 'The sanctuary model of organizational change for children's residential treatment', *Therapeutic Community: The International Journal for Therapeutic and Supportive Organizations*, 26(1): 65–81.

Boddy, J. (2023) 'Engaging with uncertainty: studying child and family welfare in precarious times', *Families, Relationships and Societies*, 12(1): 127–41.

Bovarnick, S., Peace, D., Warrington, C. and Pearce, J.J. (2018) *Being Heard: Promoting Children and Young People's Involvement in Participatory Research on Sexual Violence: Findings from an International Scoping Review*. Luton: University of Bedfordshire.

Bronfenbrenner, U. (ed) (2005) *Making Human Beings Human: Bioecological Perspectives on Human Development*. California, CA: Sage Publications.

Brown, L. (2015) 'A lasting legacy? Sustaining innovation in a social work context', *British Journal of Social Work*, 45(1): 138–52.

Brown, L. (2021) 'Managing evidence and cultural adaptation in the international transfer of innovative social work models', *International Social Work*, 64(2): 175–186.

Brown, K. and Osborne, S.P. (2012) *Managing Change and Innovation in Public Service Organizations*. London: Routledge.

Brown, L. and Osborne, S.P. (2013) 'Risk and innovation', *Public Management Review*, 15(2): 186–208.

Castro, F.G., Barrera, M. and Martinez, C.R. (2004) 'The cultural adaptation of prevention interventions: resolving tensions between fidelity and fit', *Prevention Science*, 5(1): 41–5.

Castro, F.G., Barrerra, M. and Steiker, L.K.H. (2010) 'Issues and challenges in the design of culturally adapted evidence-based interventions', *Annual Review of Clinical Psychology*, 6(1): 213–39.

Centre for Public Impact (2021) 'What we're learning about reimagining government', 27 April. Available at: www.centre forpublicimpact.org/insights/what-we-re-learning-about-reim agining-government (accessed 3 October 2023).

Clare, B. (2007) 'Promoting deep learning: a teaching, learning and assessment endeavour', *Social Work Education*, 26(5): 433–46.

Cockbain, E. (2023) 'Not even Suella Braverman's own department agrees with her about "grooming gangs"', *The Guardian*, 4 April. Available at: www.theguardian.com/commentisfree/2023/apr/04/suella-braverman-grooming-gangs-child-sexual-abuse-home-secretary-prejudice (accessed 3 October 2023).

Coliandris, G. (2015) 'County lines and wicked problems: exploring the need for improved policing approaches to vulnerability and early intervention', *Australasian Policing*, 7(2): 25–36.

Coomer, R. and Moyle, L. (2017) 'The changing shape of street-level heroin and crack supply in England: commuting, holidaying and cuckooing drug dealers across "county lines"', *British Journal of Criminology*, 58(6): 1323–42.

Cooper, A. and Lees, A. (2015) 'Spotlight: defences against anxiety in contemporary human service organizations', in D. Armstrong and M. Rustin (eds) *Social Defences against Anxiety: Explorations in a Paradigm*. London: Karnac, pp 239–55.

Costello, G.J., Conboy, K. and Donnellan, B. (2011) 'An ecological perspective on innovation management', 14th Annual IAM Conference, 31 August–2 September, Dublin: National College of Ireland.

Department for Business, Energy and Industrial Strategy (2021) 'UK innovation strategy: leading the future by creating it'. Available at: www.gov.uk/government/publications/uk-innovation-strat egy-leading-the-future-by-creating-it (accessed 3 October 2023).

Department for Children, Schools and Families (2009) *Safeguarding Children and Young People from Sexual Exploitation*. London: HMSO.

Department for Education (2022) 'Children's social care innovation programme: insights and evaluation'. Available at: www.gov.uk/guidance/childrens-social-care-innovation-programme-insights-and-evaluation (accessed 3 October 2023).

Department for Education (2023) *Stable Homes, Built on Love: Implementation Strategy and Consultation*, Children's Social Care Reform 2023, CP 780. London: Department for Education.

Dettlaff, A.J., Weber, K., Pendleton, M., Boyd, R., Bettencourt, B. and Burton, L. (2020) 'It is not a broken system, it is a system that needs to be broken: the upEND movement to abolish the child welfare system', *Journal of Public Child Welfare*, 14(5): 500–17.

DeVault, M. (2006) 'What is institutional ethnography?', *Social Problems*, 53(3): 294–98.

Dewar, C., Doucette, R. and Epstein, B. (2019) 'How continuous improvement can build a competitive edge', 6 May. Available at: www.mckinsey.com/capabilities/people-and-organizatio nal-performance/our-insights/the-organization-blog/how-con tinuous-improvement-can-build-a-competitive-edge (accessed 3 October 2023).

Diamond, M.A. (2007) 'Organizing and the analytic third: locating and attending to unconscious organizational psychodynamics', *Psychoanalysis, Culture & Society*, 12: 142–64.

Finch, J. and Schaub, J. (2015) 'Projective identification as an unconscious defence: social work, practice education and the fear of failure', in D. Armstrong and M. Rustin (eds) *Social Defences against Anxiety: Explorations in the Paradigm*. London: Karnac, pp 300–14.

Firmin, C. (2017) *Contextual Safeguarding: An Overview of the Operational, Strategic and Conceptual Framework*. Luton: University of Bedfordshire.

Firmin, C. (2018) *Abuse between Young People: A Contextual Account*. Oxford: Routledge.

Firmin, C. (2020) *Contextual Safeguarding and Child Protection: Rewriting the Rules*. Oxford: Routledge.

Firmin, C. and Lloyd, J. (2020) *Contextual Safeguarding: A 2020 Update on the Operational, Strategic and Conceptual Framework*. Luton: University of Bedfordshire.

Firmin, C. and Lloyd, J. (2022) 'Green lights and red flags: the (im) possibilities of Contextual Safeguarding responses to extra-familial harm in the UK', *Social Sciences*, 11(7): 303. Available at: https:// doi.org/10.3390/socsci11070303 (accessed 3 October 2023).

Firmin, C., Warrington, C. and Pearce, J. (2016) 'Sexual exploitation and its impact on developing sexualities and sexual relationships: the need for contextual social work interventions', *British Journal of Social Work*, 46(8): 2318–37.

Firmin, C., Lefevre, M., Huegler, N. and Peace, D. (2022) *Safeguarding Young People Beyond the Family Home: Responding to Extra-Familial Risks and Harms*. Bristol: Policy Press.

Firmin, C., Maglajlic, R., Hickle, K. and Lefevre, M. (forthcoming) '"Known to services" or "known by professionals": relationality at the core of trauma-informed responses to extra-familial harm'.

Fish, S. and Hardy, M. (2015) 'Complex issues, complex solutions: applying complexity theory in social work practice', *Nordic Social Work Research*, 5(1): 98–114.

FitzSimons, A. and McCracken, K. (2020) *Children's Social Care Innovation Programme Round 2 Final Report*. London: Department for Education.

Fixsen, D., Naoom, S., Blase, K., Friedman, R. and Wallace, F. (2005) *Implementation Research: A Synthesis of the Literature*. University of Florida.

Fixsen, D., Blase, K., Naoom, S. and Wallace, F. (2009) 'Core implementation components', *Research on Social Work Practice*, 19(5): 531–40.

Forrester, D., Westlake, D., Killian, M., Antonopoulou, V., McCann, M., Thurnham, A. et al (2018) 'A randomized controlled trial of training in motivational interviewing for child protection', *Children and Youth Services Review*, 88: 180–90.

Foundations (2023) 'Evidence-driven change making'. Available at: https://foundations.org.uk/ (accessed 3 October 2023).

Frosh, S. (2012) *A Brief Introduction to Psychoanalytic Theory*. Basingstoke: Palgrave.

Garcia, A.R., DeNard, C., Morones, S. and Eldeeb, N. (2019) 'Mitigating barriers to implementing evidence-based interventions in child welfare: lessons learned from scholars and agency directors', *Children and Youth Services Review*, 100: 313–31.

Gear, C., Eppel, E. and Koziol-Mclain, J. (2018) 'Advancing complexity theory as a qualitative research methodology', *International Journal of Qualitative Methods*, 17(1): 1–10.

Godar, R. and Botcherby, S. (2021) *Learning from the Greater Manchester Scale and Spread Programme – Spreading Innovation across a City-Region.* Dartington, Totnes. Research in Practice.

Goldsmith, L.J. (2021) 'Using framework analysis in applied qualitative research', *The Qualitative Report*, 26(6): 2061–76.

Hampson, M., Goldsmith, C. and Lefevre, M. (2021) 'Towards a framework for ethical innovation in children's social care', *Journal of Children's Services*, 16(3): 198–213.

Hanson, E. and Holmes, D. (2014) *That Difficult Age: Developing a More Effective Response to Risks in Adolescence: Evidence Scope.* Dartington, Totnes: Research in Practice.

Hanson, R.F. and Lang, J. (2016) 'A critical look at trauma-informed care among agencies and systems serving maltreated youth and their families', *Child Maltreatment*, 21(2): 95–100.

Harris, M.E. and Fallot, R.D. (2001) *Using Trauma Theory to Design Service Systems.* Hoboken, NJ: Jossey-Bass.

Hartley, J. (2006) *Innovation and Its Contribution to Improvement: A Review for Policy Makers, Policy Advisors, Managers and Researchers.* London: Department for Communities and Local Government.

Her Majesty's Government (2018) *Working Together to Safeguard Children: A Guide to Inter-Agency Working to Safeguard and Promote the Welfare of Children.* London: Stationary Office.

Hickle, K. (2019) 'Understanding trauma and its relevance to child sexual exploitation', in J. Pearce (ed) *Child Sexual Exploitation: Why Theory Matters.* Bristol: Policy Press, pp 151–72.

Hickle, K. and Lefevre, M. (2022) 'Learning to love and trust again: a relational approach to developmental trauma', in D. Holmes (ed) *Safeguarding Young People: Risk, Rights, Relationships and Resilience.* London: Jessica Kingsley, pp 159–76.

Holling, C.S. (1987) 'Simplifying the complex: the paradigms of ecological function and structure', *European Journal of Operational Research*, 30(2): 139–46.

Holmes, D. (2022) 'Transitional safeguarding: the case for change', *Practice*, 34(1): 7–23.

Holmes, D. and Bowyer, S. (2020) 'Transitional safeguarding: video blog'. Available at: www.theinnovateproject.co.uk/transitional-safeguarding (accessed 3 October 2023).

Holmes, D. and Smale, E. (2018) *Transitional Safeguarding – Adolescence to Adulthood: Strategic Briefing*. Dartington, Totnes: Research in Practice.

Holmes, D.R. and Marcus, G.E. (2008) 'Para-ethnography', in L.M. Given (ed) *The SAGE Encyclopedia of Qualitative Research Methods*. California, CA: SAGE Publications, Inc, pp 595–7.

Hudson, C.G. (2000) 'At the edge of chaos: a new paradigm for social work?', *Journal of Social Work Education*, 36(2): 215–30.

Huegler, N. and Ruch, G. (2022) 'Risk, vulnerability and complexity: transitional safeguarding as a reframing of binary perspectives', *Practice*, 34(1): 25–39.

Hunziker, S. and Blankenagel, M. (2021) *Research Design in Business and Management*. Wiesbaden: Springer Gabler.

Hurst, D.K. and Zimmerman, B.J. (1994) 'From life cycle to ecocycle: a new perspective on the growth, maturity, destruction, and renewal of complex systems', *Journal of Management Inquiry*, 3(4): 339–54.

Islam, G. (2015) 'Practitioners as theorists: para-ethnography and the collaborative study of contemporary organizations', *Organizational Research Methods*, 18(2): 231–51.

Jackson, D.B., Del Toro, J., Semenza, D.C., Testa, A. and Vaughn, M.G. (2021) 'Unpacking racial/ethnic disparities in emotional distress among adolescents during witnessed police stops', *Journal of Adolescent Health*, 69(2): 248–54.

Jesus, A. and Amaro, M.I. (forthcoming) 'The growing rhetoric of entrepreneurship in times of crisis: future challenges of social work in the case of Portugal', in J.P. Wilken, A. Parpan-Blaser, S. Prosser, S. van der Pas and E. Jansen (eds) *Social Work and Social Innovation: Emerging Trends and Challenges for Practice, Policy and Education in Europe*. Bristol: Policy Press.

Jones, R. (2018) *In Whose Interest? The Privatisation of Child Protection and Social Work*. Bristol: Policy Press.

Kaye, S., DePanfilis, D., Bright, C.L. and Fisher, C. (2012) 'Applying implementation drivers to child welfare systems change: examples from the field', *Journal of Public Child Welfare*, 6(4): 512–30.

Keathley, J., Merrill, P., Owens, T., Meggarrey, I. and Posey, K. (2013) *The Executive Guide to Innovation: Turning Good Ideas into Great Results*. Milwaukee, WI: ASQ Quality Press.

Klein, M. (1952) 'The origins of transference', *The International Journal of Psychoanalysis*, 33: 433–8.

Klein, M. (1973 [1955]) 'On identification', in M. Klein (ed), *Envy and Gratitude and Other Works 1946–1963*. London: Karnac, pp 141–75.

Laird, S.E., Morris, K., Archard, P. and Clawson, R. (2018) 'Changing practice: the possibilities and limits for reshaping social work practice', *Qualitative Social Work*, 17(4): 577–93.

Lankelly Chase Foundation (2017) 'Historical review of place-based approaches'. Available at: https://lankellychase.org.uk/wp-cont ent/uploads/2017/10/Historical-review-of-place-based-approac hes.pdf (accessed 3 October 2023).

Lawrence, G. (1977) 'Management development … some ideals, images and realities', in A.D. Coleman and M.H. Geller (eds) *Group Relations Reader*. Washington, DC: A.K. Rice Institute Series, pp 231–40.

Lefevre, M. (2023) 'Contextual Safeguarding – does it work and how would we know?'. Available at: www.theinnovateproject.co.uk/ contextual-safeguarding-does-it-work-and-how-would-we-know (accessed 5 October 2023).

Lefevre, M., Hickle, K., Luckock, B. and Ruch, G. (2017) 'Building trust with children and young people at risk of child sexual exploitation: the professional challenge', *British Journal of Social Work*, 47(8): 2456–73.

Lefevre, M., Hickle, K. and Luckock, B. (2019) '"Both/and" not "either/or": reconciling rights to protection and participation in working with child sexual exploitation', *British Journal of Social Work*, 49(7): 1837–55.

Lefevre, M., Preston, O., Hickle, K., Horan, R., Drew, H., Banerjee, R. et al (2020) *Evaluation of the Implementation of a Contextual Safeguarding System in the London Borough of Hackney*. London: Department for Education.

Lefevre, M., Hampson, M. and Goldsmith, C. (2022) 'Towards a synthesised directional map of the stages of innovation in children's social care', *British Journal of Social Work*, 53(5): 2478–98.

Lefevre, M., Holmes, L, Banerjee, R., Horan, R. and Hickle, K. (with Goldsmith, C., Paredes, F., Farieta, A., Baylis, S., Nasrawy, M., Huegler, N. and Bowyer, S.) (2023) 'Evaluation of the process and impact of embedding Contextual Safeguarding in the London Borough of Hackney'. Available at: https://theinnovateproject. co.uk/wp-content/uploads/2023/09/Evaluation-of-embedd ing-Contextual-Safeguarding-in-Hackney_Final-published.pdf (accessed 29 September 2023).

Lefevre, M., Temperley, J. and Goldsmith, C. (forthcoming) 'Creating a conducive context for innovation in children's social care'.

Lipmanowicz, H. and McCandless, K. (2013) *The Surprising Power of Liberating Structures: Simple Rules to Unleash a Culture of Innovation.* Seattle, WA: Liberating Structures Press.

Lloyd, J., Hickle, K., Owens, R. and Peace, D. (2023) 'Relationship-based practice and Contextual Safeguarding: approaches to working with young people experiencing extra-familial risk and harm', *Children and Society*. Available at: https://doi.org/10.1111/ chso.12787 (accessed 3 October 2023).

Lowe, T. and French, M. (2021) 'The HLS principles: systems', in Human Learning Systems (ed) *Human Learning Systems: Public Service for the Real World*. Cumbria: ThemPra Social Pedagogy, pp 76–96. Available at: www.centreforpublicimpact.org/assets/ documents/hls-real-world.pdf (accessed 3 October 2023).

McPheat, G. and Butler, L. (2014) 'Residential child-care agencies as learning organisations: innovation and learning from mistakes', *Social Work Education*, 33(2): 240–53.

Méndez-Fernández, A., Aguiar-Fernández, F.J., Lombardero-Posada, X., Murcia-Álvarez, E. and González-Fernández, A. (2022) 'Vicariously resilient or traumatised social workers: exploring some risk and protective factors', *British Journal of Social Work*, 52(2): 1089–109.

Menzies-Lyth, I. (1988 [1959]) 'The functions of social systems as a defence against anxiety: a report on a study of the nursing service of a general hospital', in I. Menzies-Lyth, *Containing Anxiety in Institutions: Selected Essays, Vol. I.* London: Free Association Books, pp 43–88.

Miller, E.J. and Rice, A.K. (2013) *Systems of Organization: The Control of Task and Sentient Boundaries.* Oxford: Routledge.

Moore, M. (2013) *Recognizing Public Value.* Cambridge, MA: Harvard University Press.

Mosley, J.E., Marwell, N.P. and Ybarra, M. (2019) 'How the "what works" movement is failing human service organizations, and what social work can do to fix it', *Human Service Organizations: Management, Leadership & Governance*, 43(4): 326–35.

Mulgan, G. (2014) 'Innovation in the public sector: how can public organisations better create, improve and adapt?'. Available at: https://media.nesta.org.uk/documents/innovation_in_the_public_sector-_how_can_public_organisations_better_create_improve_and_adapt_0.pdf (accessed 3 October 2023).

Mulgan, G. (2019) *Social Innovation: How Societies Find the Power to Change.* Bristol: Policy Press.

Mulgan, G. with Tucker, S., Ali, R., and Sanders, B. (2007) *Social Innovation: What It Is, Why It Matters and How It Can Be Accelerated.* Oxford: Skoll Centre for Social Entrepreneurship.

Murray, R., Caulier-Grice, J. and Mulgan, G. (2010) 'The open book of social innovation', The Young Foundation/Nesta. Available at: https://youngfoundation.org/wp-content/uploads/2012/10/The-Open-Book-of-Social-Innovationg.pdf (accessed 3 October 2023).

National Audit Office (2022) *Evaluating Innovation in Children's Social Care.* London: House of Commons.

Nesta (2016) *Using Research Evidence: A Practice Guide.* London: Nesta/Alliance for Useful Evidence.

OECD (Organisation for Economic Co-operation and Development) and Eurostat (2018) *Oslo Manual 2018: Guidelines for Collecting, Reporting and Using Data on Innovation*, 4th edn, Paris and Luxembourg: OECD Publishing and Eurostat. Available at: https://doi.org/10.1787/9789264304604-en (accessed 3 October 2023).

Oeij, P.R., Wouter van der Torre, A., Vaas, F. and Dhondt, S. (2019) 'Understanding social innovation as an innovation process: applying the innovation journey model', *Journal of Business Research*, 101: 243–54.

Office of the Chief Social Worker for Adults, Research in Practice, Association of Directors of Adult Social Services, BASW (British Association of Social Workers), Care and Health Improvement Programme and the NWG Network (2021) 'Bridging the gap: transitional safeguarding and the role of social work with adults – knowledge Briefing', Department of Health and Social Care. Available at: www.gov.uk/government/publications/bridg ing-the-gap-transitional-safeguarding-and-the-role-of-social-work-with-adults (accessed 3 October 2023).

Owens, R. (2015) 'Working together: using group relations theory to understand and rethink the interplay between administrators and social work practitioners', *Journal of Social Work Practice*, 29(2): 231–8.

Peace, D. (forthcoming) 'Contextual Safeguarding in the voluntary and community sector: opportunities and challenges'.

Pecukonis, E., Greeno, E., Hodorowicz, H., Park, H., Ting, L., Moyers, T. et al (2016) 'Teaching motivational interviewing to child welfare social work students using live supervision and standardized clients: a randomized controlled trial', *Journal of the Society for Social Work and Research*, 7(3): 479–505.

Preston-Shoot, M., Cocker, C. and Cooper, A. (2022) 'Learning from safeguarding adult reviews about Transitional Safeguarding: building an evidence base', *The Journal of Adult Protection*, 24(2): 90–101.

Rabinow, P., Marcus, G.E., Faubion, J.D. and Rees, T. (2008) *Designs for an Anthropology of the Contemporary*. Durham, NC: Duke University Press.

Radford, L., Richardson Foster, H., Barter, C. and Stanley, N. (2017) *Rapid Evidence Assessment: What Can Be Learnt from Other Jurisdictions about Preventing and Responding to Child Sexual Abuse*. Preston: University of Central Lancashire.

Rankin, J. (2017) 'Conducting analysis in institutional ethnography: guidance and cautions', *International Journal of Qualitative Methods*, 16(1): 1–11.

Reynolds, V. (2011) 'Resisting burnout with justice-doing', *The International Journal of Narrative Therapy and Community Work*, 4: 27–45.

Roberts, L., Mannay, D., Rees, A., Bayfield, H., Corliss, C., Diaz, C. et al (2021) ' "It's been a massive struggle": exploring the experiences of young people leaving care during COVID-19', *YOUNG*, 29(4_suppl): S81–99.

Rogers, E. (2003) *Diffusion of Innovations* (5th edn). New York, NY: Free Press.

Ruch, G. (2007) 'Reflective practice in contemporary social care: the role of containment', *British Journal of Social Work*, 37(4): 659–90.

Ruch, G. (2020) *Understanding the Impact of Social Systems as Defences in your Organisation*. Dartington, Totnes: Research in Practice.

Rutter, H., Savona, N., Glonti, K., Bibby, J., Cummins, S., Finegood, D.T. et al (2017) 'The need for a complex systems model of evidence for public health', *The Lancet*, 390(10112): 2602–4.

Salzberger-Wittenberg, I. (1983) 'Emotional aspects of learning', in I. Salzberger-Wittenberg, G. Henry and E. Osbourne (eds) *The Emotional Experience of Learning and Teaching*. London: Routledge and Kegan Paul, pp 53–76.

Sapiro, B., Johnson, L., Postmus, J.L. and Simmel, C. (2016) 'Supporting youth involved in domestic minor sex trafficking: divergent perspectives on youth agency', *Child Abuse and Neglect*, 58: 99–110.

Sawyer, S., Azzopardi, P., Wickremarathne, D. and Patton, G. (2018) 'The age of adolescence', *The Lancet Child and Adolescent Health*, 2(3): 223–8.

SCIE (Social Care Institute for Excellence) (2012) *Introduction to Children's Social Care*. London: Social Care Institute for Excellence.

Scottish Government (2021) 'Trauma-informed practice: a toolkit for Scotland'. Available at: www.gov.scot/publications/trauma-informed-practice-toolkit-scotland/ (accessed 3 October 2023).

Scottish Government (2023) 'Criminal exploitation: practitioner guidance'. Available at: www.gov.scot/publications/practitioner-guidance-criminal-exploitation/documents/ (accessed 3 October 2023).

Sebba, J. (with Luke, N., Rees, A. and McNeish, D.) (2017) 'Systemic conditions for innovation in children's social care. Children's social care innovation programme: thematic report 4'. Available at: www.education.ox.ac.uk/wp-content/uploads/2019/06/Systemic-conditions-for-innovation-in-childrens-social-care.pdf (accessed 3 October 2023).

Shuker, L. (2013) 'Constructs of safety for children in care affected by sexual exploitation', in M. Melrose and J. Pearce (eds) *Critical Perspectives on Child Sexual Exploitation and Trafficking*. Basingstoke: Palgrave Macmillan, pp 125–38.

Smith, D.E. (2005) *Institutional Ethnography: A Sociology for People*. Lanham, MD: AltaMira Press.

Smith, D.E. and Griffith, A.I. (2022) *Simply Institutional Ethnography: Creating a Sociology for People*. Toronto: University of Toronto Press.

Smith, H. (2019) 'Omniscience at the edge of chaos: complexity, defences and change in a children and families social work department', *Journal of Social Work Practice*, 33(4): 471–80.

Social Exclusion Unit (2005) *Transitions: Young Adults with Complex Needs*. London: Office of the Deputy Prime Minister.

Suh, E. and Holmes, L. (2022) 'A critical review of cost-effectiveness research in children's social care: what have we learnt so far?', *Social Policy and Administration*, 56(5): 742–56.

Sweeney, A., Clement, S., Filson, B. and Kennedy, A. (2016) 'Trauma-informed mental healthcare in the UK: what is it and how can we further its development?', *Mental Health Review Journal*, 21(3): 174–92.

The Promise, Scotland (2020) 'What must change: Plan 21–24'. Available at: https://thepromise.scot/what-must-change/plan-21-24 (accessed 13 October 2023).

Trevithick, P. (2014) 'Humanising managerialism: reclaiming emotional reasoning, intuition, the relationship, and knowledge and skills in social work', *Journal of Social Work Practice*, 28(3): 287–311.

Tufail, W. (2015) 'Rotherham, Rochdale, and the racialised threat of the "Muslim grooming gang"', *International Journal for Crime, Justice and Social Democracy*, 4(3): 30–43.

UK Research Integrity Office (2023) *Code of Practice for Research.* Croydon: UK Research Integrity Office.

Van der Pas, S. and Jansen, E. (forthcoming) 'Regional learning networks in the social welfare domain: drivers of social innovation in social work', in J.P. Wilken, A. Parpan-Blaser, S. Prosser, S. van der Pas and E. Jansen (eds) *Social Work and Social Innovation: Emerging Trends and Challenges for Practice, Policy and Education in Europe*. Bristol: Policy Press.

Wroe, L. (2022) 'When helping hurts: a zemiological analysis of a child protection intervention in adolescence – implications for a critical child protection studies', *Social Sciences*, 11(6): 263. Available at: https://doi.org/10.3390/socsci11060263 (accessed 3 October 2023).

Wroe, L., Peace, D., Bradbury, V. and Huegler, N. (2023) 'Contextual Safeguarding across borders: the international applicability and feasibility of Contextual Safeguarding'. Available at: www.context ualsafeguarding.org.uk/media/o4doufgz/csab-international-findi ngs-briefing.pdf (accessed 3 October 2023).

Young Foundation (2012) 'Defining social innovation, Deliverable 1.1 of the FP7-project: TEPSIE (290771)'. Available at: https:// youngfoundation.org/wp-content/uploads/2012/12/TEPSIE. D1.1.Report.DefiningSocialInnovation.Part-1-defining-social-innovation.pdf (accessed 3 October 2023).

Zuber, C.D., Alterescu, V. and Chow, M.P. (2005) 'Fail often to succeed sooner: adventures in innovation', *The Permanente Journal*, 9(4): 44–9.

Index

References to figures appear in *italic* type.

Printed in the USA
CPSIA information can be obtained
at www.ICGtesting.com
JSHW012236270224
58181JS00004B/55